Skydive

Sport Parachuting Explained

SKYDIVE

SPORT PARACHUTING EXPLAINED

Chris Donaldson

The Crowood Press

First published in 2000 by
The Crowood Press
Ramsbury, Marlborough
Wiltshire SN8 2HR

British Library Cataloguing-in-Publication Data
A catalogue record for this book is available from the British Library.

ISBN 1 86126 350 3

Dedication
I would like to dedicate this book to every student I have had the honour to
train and share an aircraft with. I have made my first jump thousands of times
through your eyes.

Acknowledgements
I would like to express my sincere thanks to the photographers who have given
this book its visual aspect: Stuart Meacock and Ron O'Brien for the formation
skydiving and ground shots; Roger Tamblyn for the CRW; Tony Danbury and
Chris Lloyd for the freestyle, freeflying and skysurfing; and Elliot Clarke for the
BASE photographs. Thanks also to Lesley for her help.

Line art by David Sawyer and Andrew Green.

Printed and bound in Great Britain by Redwood Books, Trowbridge.

Contents

Introduction

The expressions 'parachuting' and 'skydiving' regularly confuse people. For the uninitiated to see pictures or film of people skydiving – in free fall – suspended in the sky without visible means of support, is to wonder where parachutes themselves come into the equation. Likewise, to see jumpers descending under their canopies, landing softly within a target area, begs the question of how these parachutes came to be above their heads in the first place!

The truth is that the term 'skydiving' generally refers to the period before the jumper has chosen to manually open their parachute: the time when they are falling quickly through the sky, acted upon (invariably!) by the force of gravity. They are balancing on a semi-solid column of air created by their fall, and the resistance they experience is the medium they will use to control themselves.

'Parachuting' refers to the period spent under the open parachute. The drawback of free fall is that it cannot be pursued all the way to the ground! The speed, or descent rate, is simply to great for the jumper to survive. Therefore at a safe altitude, one that gives margin for any emergency procedures,

the skydiver will manually open their parachute and decelerate. They will then fly themselves safely to the ground, using the aerodynamic characteristics of the parachute instead of those of their arms and legs.

The aim of this book is simply to de-mystify our sport and explain why, and how, thousands of men and women around the world today, and in past decades, have managed to pursue this activity regularly and safely. It will chart the skills taught to ensure that we don't just barely escape with

our lives every time we jump, but somehow manage to relax within a very dramatic environment, and enjoy our chosen recreation.

Even so, it will always be hard to describe in narrative the simple power of free fall. The sheer joy of falling at 120mph down the side of a developing cumulus cloud, the circular rainbows on the vapour below, while around you, your friends perform back loops and rolls in the cold air. How the roar of a powerful turbine engine quickly fades as you dive through the open door, and the

planet spreads out below you, impossibly big.

Skydiving happens in most countries of the world, and while some nations still pursue the sport within a mainly military framework, the progression from novice to expert follows a similar format wherever you go. The equipment used is also very similar. I will not, therefore, confine my explanations within the doctrine of any particular governing body. Skydiving has world-wide appeal. I hope that this book will also.

Primarily aimed at people outside the sport, i.e. potential skydivers, I hope what follows will also interest and enlighten those students who are already embarked on the progression ladder. Wherever you are, however it's going for you, stick with it. It's worth it.

Chris Donaldson

1 The Sport Today

THE SKYDIVER'S PERCEPTION

In general terms, the public perception of the type of person who would voluntarily throw themself out of an aircraft is very different from the reality. The average skydiver tends to be a level-headed individual who has simply decided to devote a great amount of their leisure time and disposable income to their chosen sport. They might just as easily have chosen to climb a mountain, sail a boat or kick a ball around a field.

By and large, these people are not daredevils, possessed of a death wish. Neither are they skydiving to prove their bravery to themselves or anybody else. Quite simply, they attend parachuting centres in order to gain as much enjoyment as possible from the sport in the time that they have available.

The same is true of professional skydivers, people who earn a living teaching the necessary skills to various levels of student parachutist. Also, it is true of the relatively few, lucky and talented individuals around the world who skydive professionally and competitively, in pursuit of the zenith of sporting achievement: a gold medal at national or world championship level.

THE NON-SKYDIVER'S PERCEPTION

Most people one meets from day to day would never dream of jumping. The reason is simple: they perceive our sport as dangerous, and do not have the motivation to research the risks involved and the safety umbrella that is thrown over every sport parachute operation. The sport itself is also guilty, historically, of failing to make itself accessible to the public in a level-headed way, and to provide the information essential to a balanced weighing of the risks.

The number of men and women that attend first jump courses around the world each year, however, is still relatively large, and the eternal problem for parachuting organisations to address is not 'How do we get people to come and make a first jump?', but 'How do we get people to continue after their first jump?'

A great number of the individuals that continue in the sport do so for different reasons than the ones they had for booking on a first jump course. The initial motivation may well have been that they were looking for a new outlet for their adventurous leanings, or maybe some activity to fill a 'gap' in their leisure time. It is just as likely, however, to have been because they were part of a group of friends that had decided to go and scare themselves silly for a weekend! They will approach the sport of parachuting with the same sense of anticipation and foreboding that they would a high-adrenaline fairground ride.

There is nothing whatsoever wrong with this approach. The staff of any parachute school will teach the same skills and attitude regardless of an individual's motivation. However, for someone to continue, weekend after weekend, and to nurture a desire to progress through all the stages of learning, in spite of adverse weather, in spite of a failure to perform their exercises perfectly every time, a greater commitment is needed than the desire for a quick 'adrenaline fix'.

- Skydiving will not ever help you overcome your fear of heights.

- Skydiving in a recreational environment has no purpose whatsoever, other than enjoyment for its own sake.

- Skydiving is, by its nature, initially very scary. The only way to reduce this fear is to skydive as much as you can in the early stages, and to take account of every word of instruction that is given to you by a qualified person.

THE DROP ZONE

Let us first of all define the term 'drop zone' or 'DZ'. In legal terms, the drop zone is an area of sky and ground around a parachuting airfield in which skydiving and parachuting may be expected to take place. In day-to-day parlance, the drop zone is defined as the parachute centre itself. Drop zones range in size and scale. There are small weekend concerns that may operate on a club basis, where everyone is a member and helps with the day-to-day running. Alternatively there are large, full-time commercial centres employing a number of professional staff. The size of a parachute centre bears no relation to its efficiency or ability to run a safe operation.

Subsequent chapters will deal with the minutiae of drop zone life: the various disciplines that one can see practised there; the student training programme experienced jumpers rehearsing their manoeuvres on the ground; the equipment and the packing process. First of all, however, an overview of a busy parachute centre and the individuals you may meet there.

A busy day at the drop zone.

THE CHIEF INSTRUCTOR

The Centre Chief Instructor, or CCI as he or she is generally known, is in overall charge of the day-to-day safe running of any parachuting operation, large or small. They will be a very experienced skydiver, and most national bodies require them to have qualifications beyond that of a normal instructor. Quite apart from any qualifications on paper, however, a great deal of time in the sport is a necessary factor. Situations can arise in which decisions are made by a CCI that are based purely on years spent observing and reacting to real situations.

In the framework of a small weekend centre, the CCI may be forced to have their finger in every pie. They may deal with some of the student training. They may be involved in the packing of the club's parachutes. They may even re-fuel the aircraft!

At a larger, commercial centre, with many different activities occurring simultaneously, the CCI will invariably delegate duties to a qualified and numerous staff. This will enable them to retain an overview of the operation. A good analogy is that of a skipper on board ship. He or she will direct things to be done, without the distraction of having to do them personally. Having said that, a good CCI will remain accessible to staff and customers alike. They are also much more likely to gain respect if they are seen to be a current skydiver.

INSTRUCTOR

The role of an instructor changes as a skydiver progresses through the sport. Initially, these are the people who will teach the ground school of your first jump course. They will do their utmost, not just to prepare you physically for your first jump, but also to enthuse you with the vibrancy of the sport. Any latent enthusiasm that a student has must be more than matched by the person who is teaching them. Attitude is as important as ability. An instructor will have undergone a training process lasting many months. This will have been overseen by a national governing body, and the instructor examined by individuals independent of their own drop zone.

As a student returns to continue their parachuting career, having made the all-important decision that their first jump will not be their last, the instructor becomes a coach. All the skills that must be learned on the road to becoming an experienced skydiver must be taught carefully and in the proper sequence. An instructor will regularly face a conflict of enthusiasm versus ability within a student. Only their experience and integrity stands between the over-eager participant and a potential accident. As with all teachers throughout history, instructors sometimes disappoint as much as they inspire.

As an intermediate skydiver becomes experienced, they leave the instructional 'umbrella'. They are now probably qualified to pack their own equipment. They can skydive unsupervised from altitude with their contemporaries, and they have left behind any formal instruction on the basic survival skills. The instructor's role at most centres now changes. They will simply assist in the smooth running of the drop zone in order to provide a facility for these people to come and jump. They will, however, play their part in observing any breach of the current rules and regulations. On occasion, an individual's or group's natural enthusiasm may play a little loose with safety procedures; it is then the instructor's job to bring things back under control in the most low-key way possible. Safety is the only thing that comes before fun.

THE PILOT

The pilot's job is to fly the aircraft. No surprise there then! Seriously, with the exception of certain extreme skydiving-related activities, there can be no skydiving or parachuting without the means to carry the participants to altitude. The aircraft, whatever type or size, is the base from which we pursue our sport. Our time spent inside the aircraft is usually boring, sometimes scenic, and periodically cold. But it is always necessary.

No one's role at a drop zone is as important as the pilot's. Skydivers expect to leave the aircraft at the correct point over the ground. This is essential in order that they may land in the designated landing area. It is the pilot's job to fly the aircraft sufficiently accurately that this is consistently achieved. Aviation is a costly business, and the costs that a centre passes on to its customers and students are related directly to the price of aviation fuel. It is therefore important that the aircraft is in the correct place, at the correct altitude, at the correct time. This is no mean feat, and a good 'jump pilot' is a precious commodity. In any aircraft emergency, the pilot remains in control of the aircraft, and liaises with the parachutists to gain the best possible outcome.

The pilot may be a skydiver, but not necessarily so. Many pilots use the hours amassed at parachute centre to gain ratings outside the sport in subsequent years.

THE MANIFESTOR

A group of parachutists or skydivers preparing to go airborne together constitutes a 'lift'. This may comprise a party of students with their instructor, or a number of experienced jumpers going to altitude in order to take part in any one of a number of different disciplines.

The manifestor is the person responsible for compiling on the 'manifest' form the names of the jumpers on a particular lift and details of what they intend to do in the air, and making sure that they are qualified to perform their chosen tasks. In most countries, parachuting law states that one copy of the manifest goes to the aircraft and that one remains on the ground. The manifest will be used to brief the pilot on the altitude to fly to, the number of runs to make over the target area, and the numbers of jumpers exiting on each run.

The manifest board is normally the first port of call for jumpers arriving at the parachute centre. Most centres operate on a first come, first served basis. On a sunny morning therefore, it is not unusual to see a queue developing before the manifest is officially open.

The efficiency of the manifest is directly related to the productivity of the parachute centre. A well-run manifest will ensure that the centre runs economically and that each jumper or team spends maximum time in the air. An inefficient manifest means that there will be frequent delays and that the aircraft may have to be shut down between lifts while a problem is sorted out. This can lead to frustration as jumpers sit on the ground watching precious minutes (or hours!) of good weather roll by.

The manifestor must be Gunga Din, able to keep their head when all about them are losing theirs. At some centres, it is the least envied job.

THE DROP ZONE CONTROLLER

If any one at a parachute centre needs to know precisely what is happening to who, at any given time, it is the drop zone controller,

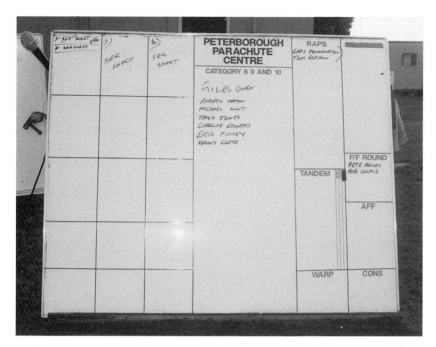

The manifest board on a quiet day.

or 'DZ controller'. Normally an instructor designated by the CCI, the DZ controller is responsible, amongst other things, for observing all parachuting and skydiving during the day. If an incident occurs, such as a landing injury, it must be noted immediately and usually a vehicle despatched with first aid on board.

The DZ controller will normally have a set of telemeters – powerful, tripod-mounted binoculars – with which to observe everything. Sometimes, a free-fall exercise will need to be seen and critiqued from the ground. The altitude and distance from the observer is usually such that telemeters are essential.

In the case of a lift of twenty or more skydivers exiting a large aircraft at up to 15,000ft (4,500m), it is impossible (and unnecessary) to watch everyone in free fall. Therefore, the DZ controller will count the canopies as they open, thus accounting for everyone, and watch them throughout their canopy ride to the ground.

Drop zone control.

The DZ controller's other duties include:

- Radio communications with the jump aircraft. Each pass over the target has to be cleared from the ground so that conflict with other air traffic can be avoided.

- Liaison with the pilot and manifestor regarding the need for aircraft re-fuelling and/or maintenance.

- Reporting any notable incidents to the CCI.

We can see from all of the above that parachuting and skydiving are not organized in a haphazard fashion. Our sport differs from other outdoor adventure pursuits, such as rock-climbing or hang-gliding, for example, because it must take place within a continuously monitored environment. This in no way detracts from the sense of freedom that accompanies every skydive. It should, however, reassure its participants that help and advice are never far away.

2   A Brief History

Parachuting has enjoyed a strange, cyclic history. Initially performed for its own sake, for enjoyment or experimentation, it then became a means of transport for countless airborne troops. Although still used extensively for this purpose, it has once again reverted to its recreational form, although, as we will see, without the degree of trial and error that accompanied its earliest days.

LEGEND AND FACT

Nobody knows exactly when, or by whom, the first parachute descent was made. Legends exist of the Chinese Emperor Shun who ruled in the second century BC. He is reputed to have escaped an assassination attempt by his father by jumping from a tower supported only by two reed hats. Hardly recreation, probably not even fact, but every history must start somewhere.

In the fifteenth century, the sketches of an un-named Italian engineer show a parachute-like device, apparently capable of lowering a man to the ground. At the same time Leonardo Da Vinci produced drawings of a similar pyramid-like device with the following annotation:

> If a man have a tent roof of caulked linen, twelve braccia broad and twelve braccia high, he will be able to let himself fall from any great height without danger to himself.

Oh really? Artisans the world over have since had reason to be grateful that Da Vinci never put his design to the test.

After all, apart from buildings – that were not notably tall in those days – there was no 'great height' to descend from: air travel of any sort had yet to be invented. In the eighteenth century the Mongolfier brothers sent aloft a linen balloon filled with hot air that they heated with a fire from below. Shortly afterwards, in Paris, Jacques Charles and the Robert brothers launched a balloon filled with the recently discovered hydrogen gas. This device was apparently destroyed by locals upon landing, who assumed it to be the work of the Devil. The Mongolfier brothers, not to be outdone, launched a sheep, a duck, and a cockerel under one of their early balloons, all of whom landed safely.

A milestone was passed in 1783, when Pilatre de Rozier and the Marquis D'Arlandes became the first humans to be hoisted airborne, in a cradle hung beneath their hot air balloon. They achieved a reputed altitude of 3,000ft (900m) and, once again, landed without injury. It seems strange then, that as soon as man had achieved a basic knowledge of balloons, he started to devise all kinds of ways to jump off or out of them!

Despite various contenders, we can probably credit another Frenchman, Louis Sebastian Lenormand with the invention of the parachute roughly as we know it. He produced a canopy made of linen, 6ft (1.8m) deep and 14ft (4.3m) wide, strengthened at its 'periphery' (edge) and equipped with a number of rigging lines that held a wicker basket slung below the whole assembly. As primitive as this parachute was, it is fundamentally similar in design to the round canopies used today. Once again, it was left to the animal kingdom to assume the roll of test pilot, and several domestic creatures were dropped successfully from an observatory tower at Montpelier. Although, like many of the early designers, many of whom tried to take credit for his invention, Lenormand did not trust his canopy with a human cargo. He was, however, the first man to call the device a 'parachute'.

The first undoubted intentional parachute descent by a human being was made by André-Jacques Garnerin. (The French didn't have a monopoly on these early designs and attempts, though they were certainly the most flamboyant.) Garnerin had previously flown in balloons himself, both as a passenger and pilot, and had fought for the French revolutionary army. He was imprisoned for three years by the Austrians in Hungary, and it was here, some say, that he hit upon the idea of escape from his lofty cell by parachute. On gaining his freedom, he returned to France and began construction of a parachute that bore more than a passing resemblance to Lenormand's design. We are not certain of the exact dimensions of his canopy, but conjecture has it at about 32ft (10m) in diameter, and constructed of cotton sailcloth, lined with paper. The lining was designed to decrease the porosity of the fabric, and so lessen the descent rate. A small circular piece of wood was installed in the 'apex' (top) of the parachute, and further down inside, a wooden hoop, 8ft (2m) in diameter was sewn into the fabric. When the assembly was eventually suspended below the

balloon cradle, this innovation would hold the lower periphery open, and the canopy would inflate more quickly. From the lower hem, thirty-six lines of braided cord, 30ft (9m) in length, ran down to a wicker basket that would hold the intrepid parachutist.

Going completely against tradition, Garnerin declined to test the parachute using domestic animals or livestock of any sort! The probable motivation for this was simply glory. These early pioneers had learned to work a crowd, and had become alert to the possibility of financial gain from their endeavours and exhibitions. Garnerin decided to test the parachute himself, and in June 1797, a paying crowd gathered in the Jardin de Byron in Paris, to witness the first manned parachute descent.

It failed.

The hydrogen balloon did not contain enough of the gas to allow it to lift, and Garnerin's embarrassment was matched only by the ridicule of the crowd and assembled press. They had to wait another four months before Garnerin was ready to try again. Fortunately the wait proved worth it. At five o'clock in the afternoon, 22 October, the balloon lifted to a height of 2,000ft (600m) supporting both parachute and Garnerin, who was standing in the basket. He cut the rope that held him to the balloon ... and parachuting was born. Apparently the canopy developed quickly and without incident, and though the basket was subject to some wild oscillations as the canopy spilled air, Garnerin landed safely, his reputation with his public restored.

Over the next few years, Garnerin continued to display his balloons and parachutes, albeit only occasionally. He probably reckoned that his odds of survival were greater if he did not regularly display his impudence to the skygods! He did, however,

André-Jacques Garnerin descends from the skies.

persuade one other to attempt parachuting. This was a certain Mademoiselle Jeanne Labrosse, who jumped from one of Garnerin's balloons in 1799. She, too, landed safely, and Garnerin showed his gratitude by marrying her.

The next pioneer of note was Robert Cocking, an Englishman. He took to the air in 1836 using a radically different design that conformed to a line of thinking popular amongst some of the early parachute designers. They took the familiar dome-shaped canopy and quite literally turned it on its head! The major problem encountered by Garnerin and his associates during the actual descent was that of oscillation. A round, or cone-shaped parachute is basically a drag device. It traps air because of the jumper's body weight and acts as a huge air brake. During the descent, if the air in the canopy cannot escape by other means, it will tend to spill from under the peripheral hem and tip the parachute as it does so. This will transmit an oscillation to the suspended weight, that can swing the jumper into the ground.

Robert Cocking took the ideas of the English aeronautical pioneer Sir George Cayley and the German scientist Lorenz Hengler,

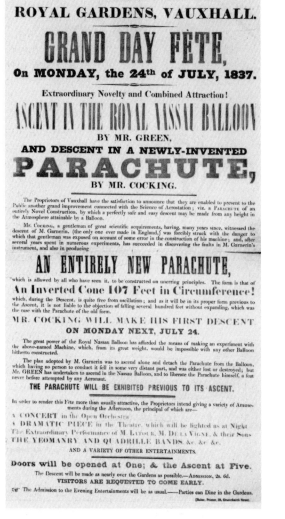

A poster advertising Robert Cocking's ill-fated descent using his 'inverted cone' parachute.

who proposed that an 'inverted cone' would provide the necessary drag for a slow descent, while continuously spilling air evenly around its shape. Cocking tested various scale models from London Bridge, and directed the construction of the device itself.

In 1836, he approached the owners of Vauxhall Gardens, who had recently completed the construction of a balloon large enough to lift the parachute, and proposed a live drop. After much deliberation and financial wrangling, it was decided to stage Cocking's first descent on 24 July 1837. Cocking was, at this time, sixty-one years old.

He was lifted to an altitude of 5,000ft (1,500m), and took two attempts to release himself from the balloon. As he did, the balloon shot upwards as the heavy assembly fell free, and for a few seconds everything went according to plan. Cocking's inverted cone began a stately descent towards the waiting crowd. Unfortunately, things went quickly wrong. Observers saw the canopy suddenly crumple, and the descent rate increase rapidly. The balloon had somehow become damaged during the release (subsequent conjecture never agreed as to why exactly this happened) and brave Robert Cocking spiralled to his death, and to a place in history as the first-ever parachuting fatality.

The inverted cone, though fine as a theoretical design, never attracted the interest to be pursued as a practical parachute. Subsequent pioneers concentrated on the more traditional, dome-shaped Garnerin design.

The latter half of the nineteenth century was the time of the show jumper. Audiences would readily pay to witness the exploits of these aerial daredevils, several of whom were elevated to 'rock star' status by public and press (the latter were never slow to give exposure to those who wrote the whole phenomena off as a recipe for certain death).

One significant advance made during this heady time was the idea of actually folding, or packing the canopy prior to its release from the balloon, as opposed to dangling the whole length below the basket. This added seconds to the deployment time, and increased the sense of drama and anticipation for the waiting crowd. A lot of the innovations of this time were introduced simply to add to the spectacle of the event, although designers were unwittingly paving the way for the time when the parachute would actually have a use and, importantly, the time when it would be used from a powered aircraft.

Charles Broadwick, an American ballooning pioneer, was probably the first person ever to design an integral assembly like those used today. He incorporated parachute, container and body harness in one unit called the 'Broadwick coat pack'. The apex of his canopy was attached, via the container, to the balloon basket by a 'static line'. Thus, as the jumper fell away, their body weight pulling against the static line caused the canopy to deploy in sequence. Contemporary designer Leo Stevens was thinking along similar lines, and developed a 'life pack', from which the static line pulled the canopy from the container via a 'ripcord'. Thus, a significant word had entered the language, one that would stay with us until the present day. The practical application of these designs led to them being proposed as a means of escape from observation balloons during wartime, but it also eventually made possible a relationship that would endure to the present day: that of parachute and powered flight.

PARACHUTING FROM AIRCRAFT

On 1 March 1912, over Kinnoch Field, Ohio, the first-ever parachute descent was made from an aeroplane in flight. It was preceded by much discussion as to the effect of the sudden loss of weight as the jumper fell away, and several test drops had been made with small canopies bearing varying loads. The pioneer parachutist was in this case Albert Berry, a professional parachute exhibitor who had answered an advertisement placed by Tom Benoist. Benoist manufactured aircraft and employed pilots to exhibit and fly them. Two of his staff had conjectured about the possibility of adding parachuting to their shows, and Benoist, although sceptical, eventually allowed tests to be carried out, providing the jumper was not one of his valuable pilots!

The aircraft used was a Benoist 'pusher', a biplane with a rear-mounted propeller. Although integral parachute systems were in their early development stages, the canopy in this case was folded into a cone beneath the lower wing, and held in place by break-ties that would allow a staged deployment. The pilot, Anthony Jannus, who had, with a colleague, suggested the whole idea, sat alongside Berry and climbed to an altitude of 1,500ft (450m). Berry then climbed out on to the axle and launched himself into the history books. He landed uneventfully and repeated his feat a couple of days later. It is interesting to note that, although this significant event was witnessed by the military, no practical application was envisioned at the time. All concerned saw it only as a means of increasing revenue at flying events and displays.

The ensuing rush to combine parachuting with powered aircraft was not embraced by all, and special mention should be made at this point of a certain Rod Law. Mr Law, a show jumper, had previously distinguished himself by jumping from the Statue of Liberty and the Bankers Trust building on Wall Street. In 1913, he decided on a further innovation, and strapped himself to a 20ft (6m) rocket armed with 50lb (23kg) of explosive. The idea was obviously to provide a means of gaining the necessary altitude for a parachute descent without having to rely on any other form of aviation. Fortunately, and surprisingly, Law survived unscathed when the rocket blew to pieces on the ground without lifting him so much as a foot!

The next development of note was the demonstration of Charlie Broadwick's 'coat pack', one of the integral harness and container systems in development at that time. It was jumped in 1914 by a diminutive female show jumper called Georgia Thompson, who parachuted under the name of 'Tiny' Broadwick, and was billed as the daughter of Charles. She was the most prolific parachutist of the time, and was reckoned to have made over a thousand jumps by the time she finished her career in 1922.

The development of the parachute temporarily stalled in America with the intrusion of the First World War, but such was the loss of life amongst aviators in the conflict, it was eventually acknowledged that the parachute might be a viable life-saver. Germany was the only power to equip her aviators with life-saving parachutes, and then only in the final stages of the conflict.

A significant milestone was passed in 1919, when Leslie Irvin became the first person to make a jump with a manually operated parachute. We have previously seen how a ripcord could be used to open a container when pulled by a static line. Irvin's system, however, had an integral handle that could be pulled by the jumper, thereby allowing them to delay the opening until they were well clear of the aircraft. Another new word entered the vocabulary, one that was to shape and define the sport as we know it today...

FREE FALL

It was widely believed by contemporary pundits that a person in a state of free fall would pass out and probably die before they ever had a chance to pull a ripcord. Thankfully this opinion was not universally held – the pioneering spirit was still strong in some quarters. Leslie Irvin had been prevented from joining the air service because of this flat feet, but his fascination with the air had encouraged him to design a static-line-operated parachute system and demonstrate it as an aerial life-saver. Through a convoluted set of circumstances, he was introduced to James Floyd Smith, who had been commissioned to design and build a parachute escape system by General Billy Mitchell. General Mitchell, unlike many of his military contemporaries, believed in the parachute as a means of airborne escape, and had lobbied for its use during the war. The problems that they encountered during their test programme related to the fact that a stricken aircraft would almost certainly be diving out of control, and therefore would not provide a suitable platform for a static-line system.

Floyd Smith built a free-fall system consisting of a backpack container closed by three ripcord pins that passed over the shoulder to a circular handle. Once this was pulled, a spring-loaded pilot chute would leap out and grab air, providing drag for a staged deployment in the same way as a static line. The difference was that the aviator could delay until they were well clear of their machine and dictate the exact moment of the pull.

On 28 April 1919 Irvin was flown to a height of 1,500ft (450m) above McCook field, Ohio. He jumped, tumbled, and pulled the ripcord. The canopy deployed perfectly and the descent was only marred by a broken ankle that Irvin sustained upon landing.

Leslie Irvin rightly won his place in the history books, but he is often credited incorrectly with the design of the system that he jumped. It came to be called the 'Irvin chute' and, although he went on to found a company – that exists to this day – to build similar designs, we must not forget that it was Floyd Smith, and not Irvin, who designed and built the original system. To say that the design stood the test of time would be an understatement. It was with a very similar system that I made my first free fall in 1977!

Incidentally, many parachutists who read this book will possibly have jumped 'Irving Skytrainers' at some time during their careers, or at least encountered the 'Irving' name on items of equipment. The spelling discrepancy comes from the first batch of headed notepaper that Irvin ordered as the 'Irvin air chute company'. The printer erred, and the 'g' was added to his name. It stuck simply because Leslie could not afford a new batch!

Throughout the 1920s and '30s, parachuting development continued. It was pursued both as a means of airborne escape, and also to serve the show jumpers who still flourished around the world. By the end of the 1930s, over 4,000 aviators had been saved by the parachute, and by the end of the Second World War this number had grown to over 100,000. Parachuting was also being used by this time to deliver troops

Leslie Irvin after the first-ever free fall, 28 April 1919.

into battle, and the development of the round canopy as a means of transport in the theatre of war is a story in itself.

There is simply not room in these pages to detail the exploits of all the brave pioneers who paved the way for the sport as we know it today. Gradually, during extended free falls, a primitive control was exerted, and some kind of stability achieved. Simultaneously, modifications were being made to canopies that enabled them to be steered. More and more people were beginning to parachute for its own sake. Not as an exhibition for financial gain, nor as a means of escape, but simply because, once separated from its inherent drama and spectacle, it was fun.

A SPORT EMERGES

The twin paths of competition parachuting and recreational 'purely for fun' parachuting emerged almost simultaneously. As early as the 1920s, the Soviet Union had backed the opening of state-run parachute centres as a means of providing the nation's youth with a character-building exercise. By 1935 there were 115 training centres and almost 11,000 people had jumped. American parachuting was progressing along slightly different lines. Accuracy landing competitions were being run with cash prizes for the most skilful jumpers ('skilful' being the operative word, as parachutes were at that time non-steerable, and control could only be exerted by pulling line groups to slip the canopy slightly).

After the Second World War, the French began to figure significantly, developing, alongside the Soviets, procedures for teaching control in free fall. Although various individuals had tried their hand at this previously, notably America's Spud Manning in the early 1930s, this was the first time that a true system had been developed. The principles of stability were introduced, and the idea of a convex, symmetrical body shape adopted for the first time. Turns were tried, experiments with fall rate and horizontal movement were carried out, and gradually man began to take control of his new environment.

Frenchman Leo Valentin and British show jumper Harry Ward took things a stage further by experimenting with winged flight. Valentin in particular deserves a special mention for his contribution to the art of free fall, and the belief that one day, with the aid of rigid wings, man would truly fly. Valentin unfortunately died at Speke airport in 1956 while demonstrating his wings at an air show.

As for the canopies, thought was also being given to increasing their control. In 1954, for the first time in a competition, a British team demonstrated a 'blank gore' modification. This entailed the removal of a single panel – or 'gore' – from the back of the canopy. The air that then escaped would provide limited thrust, and the direction could be controlled by pulling steering lines attached to the bottom of the blank gore. Unfortunately, at that particular competition, the innovation did not prove very effective, and the technique of slipping with lift webs still won the day. Nevertheless, subsequent modification proved to be more successful. Two L-shaped slots in the rear of the canopy gave increased drive and the ability to 'hold' the wind. Joining them across the bottom in a 'TU' modification gave increased turning capability. Parachutes gradually began to have the control that their pilots desired. Note the use of the word 'modification'. All these innovations were only changes to an existing design. It was not until 1961 that Pierre Lemoigne designed the first steerable parachute from scratch. It was called the Para-sail, and along with

Harry Ward and his 'wings'.

its American derivative, the Para-commander, set a new standard in canopy control. These canopies were made of a lower porosity material than their predecessors, and had a partially inverted apex that maximized the use of high-pressure air trapped within the canopy. The steering toggles could be used for braking and descent rate control as well as for turning. These canopies quickly became standard equipment for experienced and competition jumpers.

The final major progression in canopy design was one that has stayed with us until the present day, and one that we shall examine in detail in subsequent chapters. In 1964, Domina Jalbert filed a patent for the Para-foil, an inflatable wing that would change the world of parachuting forever. Although not introduced commercially until 1970, and even then treated with great suspicion by the marketplace, the ram-air, or 'square' canopy is now the canopy of choice for just about every skydiver in the world.

Clubs and centres began to organize and multiply. National governing bodies were founded to liaise with civil aviation authorities, and gradually our sport began to gain a guarded respect in the eyes of the public. During the 1970s, with the increasing accessibility of air travel, skydivers began to move around the world independently. Whereas previously just a privileged few had competed internationally, now we could all take a skydiving holiday just about anywhere we wanted. A world-wide sporting community has grown of like-minded men and women who skydive just for the fun of it. The pioneering exploits of the early jumpers reflected the spirit of the age and a need for adventurous release – in that respect nothing has changed, and we owe them a huge debt.

3 Equipment

Arguably, the only item of equipment that a skydiver needs to pursue their sport is their body! As we will subsequently see, all free-fall manoeuvres in all disciplines of the sport are performed using our arms, legs, and torsos. However, at the risk of stating the obvious, in order to skydive more than once, a jumper will need to wear, and be securely attached to, at least one parachute.

In fact, all sport parachutists around the world these days routinely jump with two packed parachutes. The main parachute is the one that will normally be used on every jump. After a free fall, the main will be manually deployed and the jumper will ride it to the ground. If ever the main parachute fails to inflate correctly – a condition known as a malfunction – then the jumper will jettison the main and deploy their reserve parachute. Both these parachutes are packed into a harness container system that is fitted securely before each jump. This container system/parachute unit, looking for all the world like a hi-tech rucksack, is generically known as a 'rig'.

In addition to their rig, all parachutists/skydivers use several pieces of ancillary or personal equipment. These include such items as altimeters, jumpsuits, helmets and goggles. We will examine the function of these in turn. However, let us first turn to the most prized possession of any skydiver. The item in which they will have invested a considerable amount of money, and the device that will save their life every time they step out of an aircraft. The combination of main and reserve canopy packed into a common harness/container system that we call the rig.

Kitted up and ready to go: front view.

Kitted up and ready to go: rear view.

THE PARACHUTES

The parachutes used by almost all intermediate and experienced skydivers, and by most students, fall into the category often referred to as 'square' but more properly called 'ram-air'. This refers to the manner in which the parachute opens and flies. In past decades, a revolution has occurred in the design of parachuting canopies. Years ago, one could have expected to jump a device referred to as a 'round' or 'drag' parachute. This is, in many instances, the traditional image of the sport: jumpers descending to earth underneath large, round umbrella-shaped canopies, pulling on con-

trol lines in order to direct the canopy's limited speed towards a given target. Although these round canopies could be flown with great accuracy in the hands of a competent pilot, their performance, in terms of forward speed and manoeuvrability, was limited by their very design.

Today, one is only likely to see round canopies used by some parachute schools for their novice jumpers. Such has been the improvement in the design and reliability of the modern ram-air canopy, that most schools will teach their students to fly one from the first jump onwards. This revolution has been resisted in some schools on the basis that a high-performance canopy can more easily be mishandled, and that emergency procedures tend to be more involved. While these arguments undoubtedly had some validity a number of years ago, they are irrelevant today as training methods, quality of instruction and superior equipment all play their part to ensure a high standard of safety. We will confine our

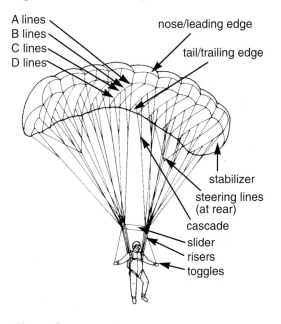

The modern ram-air canopy.

25

examination of parachute canopies to ram-air equipment.

RAM-AIR CANOPIES – DESIGN AND FUNCTION

Initially developed by Domina Jalbert in the 1960s, ram-air design was adopted and tested by sport parachute manufacturers as an alternative to round canopies. The first commercial ram-air canopies found their way on to the market in the early 1970s, and although their design bears little resemblance to the canopies of today, the theory of flight remains the same.

As the opening canopy leaves its deployment bag (*see* page 35), the jumper's suspended weight causes it to inflate into such a shape that its cross-section resembles that of an aerofoil. This is the same shape as the cross-section of a glider's wing, or that of a powered aircraft. The ram-air canopy holds its shape for two reasons.

Firstly, it is of double-skin construction. The top and bottom skins are joined at the back – the 'trailing edge' – and also along the span of the wing. The front, or 'leading edge', of the canopy is open to the air, and the span of the canopy is divided into pockets called cells.

Secondly, the suspension lines that join the jumper to the canopy are shorter at the leading edge than at the trailing edge. This causes the aerofoil to be tilted forwards, and gives it an 'angle of attack'. As the jumper's suspended weight pulls down on the canopy, it is forced to plane forwards and down. Air is therefore continually being rammed into the cells.

As jumper and parachute move forward through the air, the leading edge of the canopy breaks the air that it meets. Air moving relative to the canopy travels both above the top skin and below the bottom skin. Because the top skin is designed with a convex curve, the air flowing over it is forced to travel faster than the air flowing

A ram-air canopy from the front. All nine cells are inflated and pressurized.

under the lower skin. Fast-moving air creates low pressure on the top surface, and the canopy and its suspended weight are literally drawn towards that low pressure air by the higher-pressure air below the lower skin. Lift has been created, the canopy is flying.

In the sport of paragliding, very large ram-air canopies are used, and the fact that these canopies never have to open in free fall means that they can be designed so efficiently as to actually ascend. Paragliders will use the thermal lift of the earth or the updraughts of ridges in order to overcome the force of gravity. They can stay aloft for extended periods and travel great distances across country.

Parachutes designed for use within the sport of skydiving however, have limiting criteria:

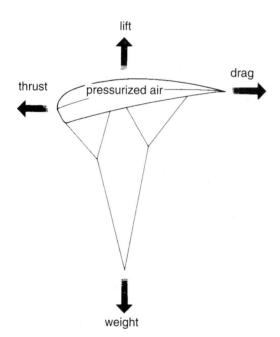

The forces acting upon a ram-air canopy in flight.

- The canopy must be small enough to enable it to be packed to a manageable size.

- The canopy must be able to open from a packed state to that of an open canopy, in four seconds flat, exposed to a 120mph (200km/h) vertical airflow.

All of this means that parachuting canopies can never be as truly efficient at creating lift as their larger relatives. Except on very rare occasions when thermal lift actually halts a descent temporarily, we are continually descending towards the earth. Contrary to what one might expect, skydivers consider this essential! Modern canopies have a very high forward speed in straight and level flight of about 30mph (50km/h) in the case of high-performance machines – they can bank, dive and spiral very quickly and, as we shall see, can be braked or 'flared' in order to skim the ground dramatically and at speed prior to landing.

They have, in short, all the qualities that a modern skydiver wants.

As we will see, within these design criteria, modern canopy manufacturers have a lot of scope to tailor the design of a particular wing so that it satisfies the requirements of any parachutist. Different disciplines require different flight characteristics and students require canopies that handle in a more docile fashion to those of the expert. In terms of general handling however, all ram-air canopies operate on the same principles. Let us examine these.

MATERIALS

The materials from which canopies are constructed are constantly changing. The early round canopies, such as the 24ft and 28ft emergency parachutes (that were later modified for sport use) were constructed of silk. This versatile material gave the canopies a small pack volume while also providing the strength and elasticity needed to survive a fast opening. As design progressed, however, silk was replaced with nylon because of its greater durability. A nylon parachute is also more resistant to damp atmospheric (and storage) conditions, and moisture in general.

Most of the nylon manufactured for sport parachuting today is termed 'ripstop'. This can also be found in many leisure garments because of its ability to resist tearing and minor damage. A panel of 'ripstop' is constructed of many small squares that are inherent to the weave. Any damage occurring within one of these squares will tend to be contained inside it. This material has advantages over the alternative plain weave that, however strong, will allow damage to travel as force and strain are applied. Damage occurring in use can therefore go from bad to worse, sometimes making a manageable situation dangerous.

The lines that attach the jumper to the canopy itself also need to tread the line between strength, elasticity and drag. Manufacturers are constantly pursuing test programmes that aim to improve the quality of their products. Synthetics such as Dacron, Kevlar and Spectra have all been, and continue to be, part of an evolution that seeks constantly to increase strength while at the same time reducing the overall weight on the skydiver's back.

Parachute nylon, like any woven fabric, will always have to cope with porosity. That is, the amount of air that will pass through the weave during the opening and subsequent descent. The greater the porosity, the more air is allowed through, the more the canopy's potential for lift is decreased, and so the more its descent rate will increase. Porosity will generally increase with age, and this, in turn, will determine the life of the parachute.

In recent years, zero porosity ('ZP') nylon has been introduced to the market. It is slippy to the touch, feeling almost like a plastic bag. Although this material is not completely zero porosity, it allows only a fraction of the air through that conventional ripstop does. The advantage here is that a canopy constructed of ZP will act more like a solid wing. It will allow almost no air through the weave during flight, making the parachute more efficient, and producing more lift for every cubic inch of pressure in the cells. In terms of performance, this simply means that the parachute will fly faster, turn more responsively and land more efficiently. Zero porosity fabric also means that a heavier parachutist can jump a smaller canopy.

Parachutes perform according to how they are 'loaded'. The greater weight beneath them, the greater the pressure in the individual cells. Although all canopies and manufacturers differ, the general rule of thumb is one pound of parachutist to every square foot of canopy. Therefore a skydiver weighing 170lb could safely jump a parachute of 170sq ft minimum area. They could jump a larger canopy quite safely, though the pressure in the cells would be less, and the overall forward speed of the parachute would be reduced. If they jumped a smaller canopy, they would find the forward speed and general performance increased, but they would have exceeded the manufacturer's 'all-up suspended weight' and may find the canopy difficult to land softly using conventional techniques.

Modern design, and particularly the introduction of ZP material, is turning this weight/area equation on its head. Skydivers can now jump smaller, more 'radical' canopies than ever before. In the early 1980s the average size of a performance parachute was probably about 220sq ft.

Today, there are canopies out there as small as 70sq ft. While use of these canopies is confined to the expert, the technology and techniques that have produced them have revolutionized the equipment market for skydivers of all levels of experience.

PARACHUTE HANDLING

We will shortly examine the differences between an experienced jumper's canopy and that of the student. Let us first, however, look at general principles of canopy handling.

Straight Ahead Flight

Just above the parachutist's shoulders, on their right and left, are located their steering toggles. These are usually soft nylon loops through which the jumper can insert their fingers with ease. The steering toggles are in turn attached to the steering, or brake, lines. Through a series of spreading suspension lines ('cascades') the jumper now has a direct attachment to the trailing edge of the canopy. Comparing the parachute again to a rigid aircraft wing, this is where the ailerons are located.

Pulling down on both toggles equally will distort the trailing edge. The canopy will slow progressively as the toggles are further depressed. Let us assume that a canopy has a forward speed of 20mph (32km/h). This is its 'full drive' speed with the steering toggles all the way up. There is no distortion to the aerofoil at this point and the canopy is flying as cleanly and as fast as possible. If the parachutist chooses to depress both toggles to about chest level, the back of the wing will have distorted somewhat. The air travelling over the upper surface is breaking from the wing before it reaches the back and the canopy's airspeed will have slowed to about 10mph (16km/h). The descent rate will have also lessened somewhat. This is known as 'half brakes'.

Flying the canopy on half brakes.

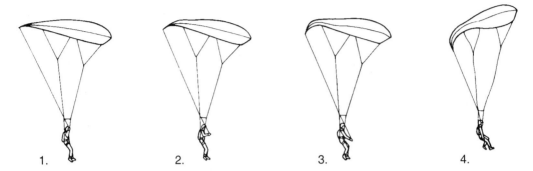

Ram-air control range: 1, full drive; 2, half brakes; 3, full brakes; 4, stall!

By the time both toggles are depressed to the waist or hip area, 'full brakes' will have been applied. The airspeed is now very low and the descent rate is starting to increase. In fact, the canopy is so distorted that it is struggling to remain aerodynamic. The upper surface airflow is such that, while some canopies are relatively stable in this mode, some are definitely not.

The Stall

Most canopies are designed and rigged so that on full drive, as we have seen, the wing is not distorted and will fly as fast as possible. The trade-off for this performance is at the other end of the control range. With both arms fully extended down past the 'full brakes' position, the canopy will distort so much that it cannot fly at all, nor can it hold the air that it contains. It will rock backwards and a 'stall' will occur. Most people have heard the phrase in connection with an aircraft or solid wing. If, during flight, a pilot decreases airspeed to such an extent that the basic principles of aerodynamic flight cease to apply, the aircraft will simply drop out of the sky. This can occur through accident or design! Aerobatic aircraft will routinely be stalled during displays when there is sufficient height to regain airspeed

and recover. On modern sport canopies, however, this is an area best avoided. Older, more docile canopies could be stalled quite safely for extended periods at altitude. Simply letting up slightly on the toggles enabled the wing to regain its shape and re-inflate. Modern canopies, however, can behave very radically during the stall and re-inflation process and malfunctions can result.

Turning the Canopy

Apart from some parachuting disciplines that require canopies to be braked as routine manoeuvres, most jumpers will quite happily fly their canopies around the sky on full drive for most of their descent (two to three minutes on average). They will use their steering toggles only to turn the parachute, and re-direct it from a particular course.

There are various types of turn possible, and these correspond to the control modes that we have already examined. With only one toggle depressed and the other left fully elevated, a 'full drive' turn is produced. One side of the canopy slows while the other remains flying at speed, and the jumper is swung out from the vertical axis as the parachute banks and turns. Turns from full drive are exhilarating, particularly on high-performance canopies. As the turn builds in speed, the jumper is progressively pressed down into their harness as the canopy attempts to overtake them vertically. How radical a turn is depends on the extent to which the toggle is depressed. With one toggle held down to the full-brake position, and the other left on full drive, one side of the canopy is virtually prevented from flying. The jumper will pendulum out level with the parachute as the speed of the turn increases.

No type of turn is possible at all without a related increase in the canopy's descent rate. If a full-drive turn is held for more than one 360-degree rotation, it is termed a 'spiral'. Spiral turns cause the parachutist to lose height very quickly indeed and they are not normally manoeuvres that you will see practised close to ground in the final stages of a descent!

Other turns are more gentle. Turns from half brakes, where one toggle is elevated and the other depressed, are flatter. The jumper remains underneath the parachute and the rate of descent increases only slightly.

Even though the average skydiver will use only full-drive turns as the norm, every jumper needs to check out and investigate all the flight characteristics of a particular parachute when it is new to them. The turn characteristics of a parachute, as well as its stall point, will vary with differing suspended weights and also, to some extent, with different atmospheric conditions.

Landing the Canopy

A parachutist will always aim to land their canopy facing into the wind. Because the opposing airflow will slow the parachute somewhat, this will make it easier for the jumper to remain on their feet. However, it will not affect their descent rate, and this

A right turn is started.

must be reduced also if a hard landing is to be avoided. A technique called a 'flare' is used in order to slow both descent rate and forward speed.

As the parachutist lines up on their final approach, they will be looking for indicators to determine the wind direction. A bright windsock will invariably be used, positioned close to the intended touchdown point. The canopy will be trimmed directly into wind using the toggles, and at a height of about 15ft (5m) both toggles will be pulled smoothly and quickly down into a deep brakes position. The effect of this manoeuvre is to convert the canopy's high forward speed into lift for a short period of time. As both speed and descent rate die away, there comes an optimum moment when they are at their least. This is the moment the parachutist aims to set their feet on the ground. Flaring the canopy correctly is an acquired technique, and split-second judgement is often the difference between looking cool and public humiliation!

- Flaring the canopy too high will mean that the 'borrowed' lift runs out before touchdown is achieved, and the canopy will sink or stall into the ground.

- Flaring the canopy too low will mean that the lift does not have enough effect and a hard landing is inevitable.

Student parachutists are usually equipped with radio receivers so that the instruction begun in the classroom can be continued through the canopy flight and specifically during the landing. They are also given canopies that, to a large extent, will forgive errors of judgement.

Experienced jumpers will possibly use a variation of this technique called a 'hook turn'. This is a skill that has evolved alongside the high-performance parachute

Starting the landing flare.

Touchdown.

revolution of the 1990s and is regarded in some quarters as a dangerous manoeuvre. Remembering that a high forward speed is necessary before the 'borrowed' lift for landing can be created, if the speed of the parachute can be artificially increased prior to landing, then the flare will be more efficient.

A turn will be introduced to the final landing approach of 90, 180, or even sometimes 360 degrees. This will increase the descent rate and forward speed accordingly, and will also increase the pressure in the cells. When the toggles are depressed for the flare, the resultant lift will be enough to make the jumper skim the ground at speed for a good distance before the speed dies away and they land. Usually the final turn will be made using the front risers (*see* page 39) in order allow a faster recovery if the turn has been made too low for safety.

It is not my intention to discuss the relative merits of the 'hook turn' in detail. Done correctly, it produces a soft, professional landing and is a valid manoeuvre. However, it should never be attempted by student or intermediate parachutists, and should never be used by an experienced jumper to compensate for a canopy that is too small for

them and could not be landed safely using a conventional technique.

DIFFERENCES BETWEEN MAIN AND RESERVE CANOPIES

Although a few parachutists still have round (drag) canopies as their reserves, the majority of jumpers today use ram-air reserve canopies. Many years ago, when ram-air design was at an earlier stage, it was common for jumpers to prefer the tried-and-tested docile characteristics of a round parachute in case of main failure. Today the world has changed. Considering that, in the event of a main canopy malfunction and the subsequent jettisoning of it in favour of the reserve, a jumper may be at a lower altitude than normal with their landing area compromised. It therefore makes sense to have a parachute that will get you out of trouble. Hence the ram-air reserve.

Main canopies today almost invariably have nine cells. This means that their span – the distance across the wing – is considerably greater than their chord – the distance

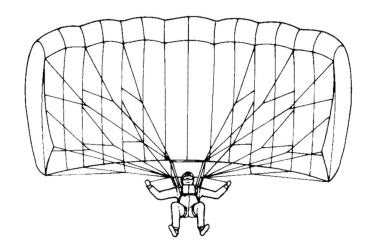

Seven-cell ram-air canopy.

*Nine-cell ram-air canopy;
wider and narrower than a
seven-cell canopy.*

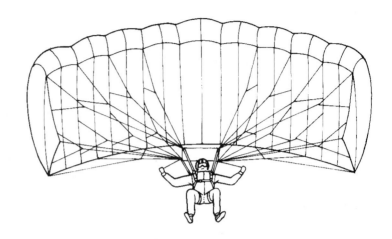

*A modern elliptical ram-air
canopy. The wing-tips are
tapered to reduce drag.*

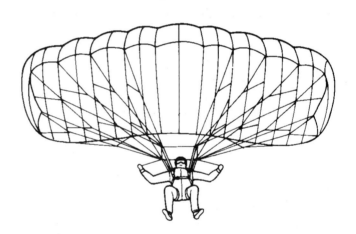

from front to back. This design feature makes then more efficient in terms of lift and gives them higher-performance turn characteristics. Some are also elliptical in shape instead of simply rectangular. This feature reduces drag at the wing-tips and makes the canopy more efficient still.

These properties are desirable in a main canopy, but can sometimes produce a fast turn on opening, or at least an off-heading canopy deployment. It can also make them less than forgiving if the jumper has a bad, or unstable, body position during the deployment sequence.

Reserve canopies are therefore usually constructed of seven cells instead of nine or more. This makes them more 'square' in appearance and less likely to display unwanted opening characteristics. This being said, manufacturers are now starting to introduce nine-cell reserves on to the market.

THE HARNESS/CONTAINER SYSTEM

In order to contain both parachutes for the aircraft ride and free fall, a skydiver wears a harness/container system. The parachute containers are located on the back in order that they will be uppermost when the skydiver deploys them.

Although there are many systems on the market, most conform to a standard set-up in terms of handle position, harness design and safety feature location. A rig is always manufactured to be as small as possible for the canopies it contains. This is to afford the jumper maximum freedom of movement in free fall and as small a weight as possible to carry around.

A parachutist will choose their harness/container system and deployment device according to their level of experience, the type of skydiving they generally practise, the safety features that the manufacturer offers, and, it has to be said, the cosmetics of the system as they see it. The average jumper will spend as much time working out a colour scheme as they will debating the other more important features of their rig. Why not? All parachute equipment is costly and, just like a motor car or set of clothing, tends to express the owner's personality!

Let us look at a typical modern rig.

THE MAIN DEPLOYMENT

There are three alternative ways to initiate the main canopy's deployment sequence. These are:

The Ripcord

Although the first and most traditional method of opening a parachute, the use of a ripcord is now generally confined to student free-fallers. It is considered safer in view of the fact that once the ripcord has been pulled, a student can regain their position and hang on to the handle while the deployment sequence occurs. They do not have to pick a precise moment to release their handle, as with the other systems we will examine. Also, the system offers less of an opportunity for entanglement if the jumper has rolled unstable – this is a possibility that must always be borne in mind with student free-fallers.

The ripcord is generally located in the small of the back on the base of the container. When it is pulled, a spring-loaded pilot chute is released into the air above the jumper's back and inflates. This in turn pulls out – via a 'bridle line' – a deployment bag containing canopy and suspension lines. The deployment and opening of the main canopy then occurs in a four-second period that we will examine shortly.

The 'Throwaway' Pilot Chute

This is the deployment system of choice for most experienced jumpers in the world today. It affords a reliable, staged and sequenced deployment while removing the bulk necessitated by a coiled metal spring.

At opening altitude, a folded pilot chute is pulled from a pocket that is located either on the base of the container like a ripcord, or in a pouch on the right-hand leg strap. This pilot chute is similar in construction to the previous type except that it has no spring. When the pilot chute has been pulled to arm's length, it is simply released into the clean free-fall airflow surrounding the jumper. It now inflates, pulling on the bridle line that in turn opens the main container by extracting a curved pin from the 'closure loop' of the container. Deployment then occurs in the normal way.

The 'Pull-Out'

This is an alternative system favoured by some experienced parachutists and generally confined to their use only. It operates as a hybrid of the two previous deployment methods and consists of a pad, again on the base of the container, which extracts both a folded pilot chute and a straight ripcord pin. Thus, the pilot chute is presented to the airflow and the container opened, simultaneously. The proponents of this system feel more directly in control of their canopy deployment and argue that there is less chance of entanglement problems if the system opens prematurely.

There will always be discussion amongst jumpers as to the best deployment system. The truth as this author sees it is that both systems are well proven to work consistently and well, and both are also prone to problems if they are subject to lack of maintenance. This is true of all parachute equipment.

THE OPENING SEQUENCE

The sequence of events that take a skydiver from the dramatic and windy state of free fall to the calmer environment of an open canopy is known as the 'opening sequence'. This happens normally in four seconds or so and at terminal velocity (*see* page 72) covers a vertical distance of some 300ft (100m). It consists of three stages:

1. Initiation;
2. Deployment;
3. Opening.

The initiation starts with the 'pull', as the jumper initiates the sequence by one of the aforementioned methods. As the pilot chute

The pilot chute is pulled.

The pilot chute pulls the deployment bag from the container.

Line stretch and opening.

gains inflation, and the bag containing the canopy is extracted from the container, the suspension lines deploy. These are not released into the air in one go, but are restrained in short 'stows' by strong elastic bands or 'bungees' on the deployment bag. This means that they stay under tension and do not become prone to knotting as they unravel. The final two stows form the 'mouth lock'. When they come under tension, the bag is pulled open, and the packed canopy is presented to the vertical airflow. Opening then occurs as the air is forced into the cells and the wing develops into the aerofoil shape we have previously seen, and starts to fly.

The sequence described here is regarded as standard throughout the parachuting world. Variations occur where a canopy may be 'free packed', that is, folded into its container without a deployment bag. This makes for a positive, but more chaotic opening and is not really compatible with modern parachute design. In the days of freefall round canopies, a sleeve was used to contain the canopy instead of a bag.

Two factors added to the opening sequence ensure that canopy deployment today is comfortable and reliable. The first of these is a device called the 'slider'. A ram-air canopy wants to develop very quickly once it is exposed to a fast airflow. At such a speed, in fact, that unless some restraint is included to slow its development, damage may occur to canopy or skydiver.

The slider is a square of nylon that is free to travel up and down the suspension lines, which pass through grommets in it in four groups. It is packed at the top with the canopy, and when the canopy opens, is forced down the lines to sit over the jumper's head. The smooth rate at which it descends during the opening sequence is a result of a conflict between the canopy's desire to force it down, and the vertical airflow's desire to keep it at the top of the lines. The canopy always wins this conflict, but the slider descent is slowed by the airflow, and the canopy opens much like a drawstring bag.

The second factor that helps the opening is the fact that the canopy is packed in half-brake mode. This simply presents a better shape to the vertical airflow for the canopy to gain its initial inflation. Normally, the first action that a jumper will take after checking their canopy is to release the brakes by pulling down on the steering toggles and releasing the stowed lines to allow full drive.

THE CUTAWAY SYSTEM

Although modern canopies are extremely reliable, the possibility of a malfunction always exists. In subsequent chapters we will examine how and why these occur. In previous decades, when low-performance parachutes were the norm, a similar reserve parachute could be deployed next to the malfunctioning main to reduce the jumper's descent rate. These parachutes were termed 'compatible' with each other and could safely be flown without danger of entanglement. Today things have changed. If a ram-air canopy malfunctions, it is likely to do so in an erratic and violent manner, and putting a reserve out next to it is inviting a canopy entanglement. Therefore, before a reserve canopy can be deployed, a 'cutaway' is necessary. The jumper must jettison their main parachute and momentarily go back into free fall before the reserve can be operated in clean air.

The word 'cutaway' always brings to mind pictures of frantic skydivers hacking away at lines with a knife as they plummet earthwards, but the truth is thankfully more efficient and considerably less dramatic!

Different devices have been used over the years to jettison the main parachute. Today, these have resolved to an industry standard, the 'three-ring release'. This device, designed by American manufacturer Bill Booth in 1976, serves as both a means of suspending the parachutist from the main canopy in normal flight, and also as a means of cutaway in the event of a malfunction. It consists of three interlocking rings, the largest ring forming part of the harness at the front of each shoulder. The two subsequent, and progressively smaller, rings are part of the 'risers', straps that connect to the suspension lines. On either side, the interlocked rings are secured by a smooth cable that travels down to a prominent pad held by Velcro on the right side of the jumpers chest. When this pad is grasped and punched firmly downwards, both cables slide through a restraining loop and the rings unlock. An immediate release from the main canopy ensues.

The reserve deployment can now be initiated.

THE RESERVE DEPLOYMENT

The reserve ripcord handle is located in a pocket on the harness at the left side of the jumper's chest, opposite to the cutaway pad. As the jumper looks down from their malfunction, both handles are immediately visible. After cutaway, the reserve handle (usually already grasped) is punched firmly down and away: this extracts the ripcord pin that holds the reserve container closed.

Now a sprung pilot chute, much the same as used to deploy student main parachutes, leaps into the fast air surrounding the falling jumper. Deployment and opening take place in more or less the same way as for a main parachute, with two important differences.

When a main parachute has fully opened, the deployment bag and pilot chute remain attached and trail above and behind the canopy. The reserve however, has a 'freebag' system. The pilot chute, bridle line and bag are totally separate from the canopy. When the reserve canopy inflates, they fly off. This is for a good reason. It is entirely possible that a parachutist cutting away will not be in a stable, or face to earth, position. The time spent getting stable may take them to a lower altitude than desirable and therefore the reserve may be deployed so that it passes past the jumper's body. The potential for entanglement is very real. However, if the pilot chute or bridle catch or wrap around the falling jumper, the canopy is free to leave the bag and open regardless of the entanglement. I have witnessed this system in use and can testify to the efficiency of its design.

The only other difference in the deployment of the reserve is that the suspension lines are stowed within a pocket on the side of the bag instead of in elastics. This speeds up the deployment and enables the canopy to be presented to the air more quickly.

I have covered the main components of an average skydiving system in some detail in the hope that it will provide a reasonable understanding of subsequent chapters as we see the equipment put to use.

PERSONAL EQUIPMENT

In addition to the rig, a skydiver will own various items of personal equipment.

Helmet

Most skydivers will wear head protection of some sort when they jump. Some national parachuting bodies allow experienced jumpers to skydive without one, reckoning that the individual can make a balanced judgement of the risks and weigh these against the sense of freedom that jumping without a helmet undoubtedly gives. Riding a fast motorbike is fun without a helmet, too, until the day the rider falls off... Free-fall collisions are always a possibility, as are hard landings in hazardous places. Also present is the chance of an engine failure on take off. All these reasons, to my mind, make the wearing of some sort of headgear good sense.

Jumpsuit

Sometimes, in warm weather, it is pleasant to skydive in a T-shirt and shorts! Almost invariably though, a jumpsuit of sorts will be worn. A student parachutist will wear a one-piece suit that will provide a consistent surface for their instructor to mount the rig on to. This will prevent the possibility of loose clothing wrapping around handles that may need to be visible at any time.

Experienced jumpers will wear whatever jumpsuit their particular discipline requires. We will examine these later.

Altimeter

All skydivers wear a visible altimeter, either on the chest strap of their harness or on their wrist. This device is basically an aneroid barometer that reacts to changes in ambient air pressure. It is calibrated in thousands of feet or meters, and can be zeroed on the ground before each jump. As the air pressure lessens on the climb to altitude, the needle rises and reads the current height above the ground. In free fall or under canopy, as the skydiver descends, it will also give them this information. Modern altimeters are robust and reliable, however, it is a foolish skydiver that places total reliance on them. As experience grows, a

'body clock' develops. This is an inbuilt sense of the time elapsed since exit and the time left to pull height. An experienced jumper will also use a visual ground reference to cross-reference this input.

The visible altimeter.

Audible altimeters have now become popular. They will be worn close to the ear and can be set to give a loud warning at various times in the latter part of a skydive, usually at 'break off' – the point at which all free-fall work ceases and the jumper finds clear air for the pull – and pull height itself, usually at around 2,500ft (750m). Most will also 'flatline' or emit a very urgent tone should the jumper still be in free fall at a perilously low altitude because of loss of awareness or a severe emergency.

All mechanical and electronic safety devices are a boon to our sport. They should always, however, be used as an aid, and never a replacement, for the personal safety and survival skills that every jumper must learn.

4   The Novice

Any sport needs a steady influx of new blood if it is to survive and grow. Skydiving is no exception, and most active drop zones around the world offer initial training and progression programmes alongside their facilities for experienced jumpers.

Although a large percentage of the people who attend these courses will only make one jump, the amount of novices who get 'the bug' is large enough to provide most parachute centres with a client base that enables them to survive commercially. This means that on an average day there will be a spread of experience on the drop zone, with students progressing at all levels.

There are three methods used to introduce novices to the sport. We will examine these in turn and look at their relative merits. When choosing which particular method is right for them, the potential parachutist needs to make a decision based on several factors, the most important of which are:

- How much money they have available to commit at the outset of their training.

- How certain they are that they will want to continue in the sport. This can be hard to judge initially because, on occasions, the desire to be a skydiver is replaced with the realization that the sport demands much time and emotional input from its participants. There are far more people who have managed one jump than there are regular skydivers.

- How much time they can devote to the sport, should they decide to continue. Parachuting demands 'currency', especially in the early stages: one jump every couple of months will not allow the novice the experience to build on previously learned skills. Also, as previously mentioned, the apprehension associated with the early stages of progression is only conquered by regular jumping.

THE STATIC LINE/FREE FALL PROGRESSION PROGRAMME

This is the route taken by most people who decide to have a go at parachuting. By taking part in a traditional 'static-line course', the novice makes their first descent on an automatically opened parachute. In an ideal world, everyone would be trained for free fall from Jump One, taught to pull their own ripcord from an ideal pull position after exit. This, however, is not realistic. As we will see, it is not just the act of pulling a ripcord that is important, but the way it is pulled and the body attitude of the skydiver. Therefore the static line is used to ensure that a canopy develops shortly after exit, no matter what.

As the novice leaves the aircraft and falls quickly away, they are affected by gravity and slipstream. Their fall takes them downwards and backwards at about 45 degrees to the aircraft door. The static line is

Static-line exit.

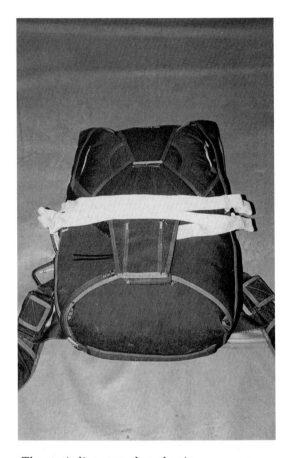

The static line stowed on the rig.

connected to a 'strongpoint' inside the aircraft and, via the parachute container, to the deployment bag containing the canopy. It quickly opens the container, pulling the bag and lines out in to the airflow. The parachutist's body weight now causes the suspension lines to stretch and the canopy is pulled out of the bag and into the fast air. From this point on the parachute develops in exactly the same manner as with a free-fall deployment, the difference being that instead of remaining attached to the top of the canopy, the deployment bag stays with the aircraft and static line. This can be pulled back inside by the instructor, who is acting as jumpmaster, and the next student made ready to jump.

Over the years, the static-line deployment system has proved itself around the world as a safe and reliable method of introducing people to the sport. Teaching will generally take place over one or two days and ideally in a small group environment. Parachuting and skydiving teaching methods do not lend themselves to a large class size. Most of the teaching is practical, and for the novice to be observed and critiqued during the course to the extent that is necessary, skills have to be practised on a one-to-one basis. In situations where a larger

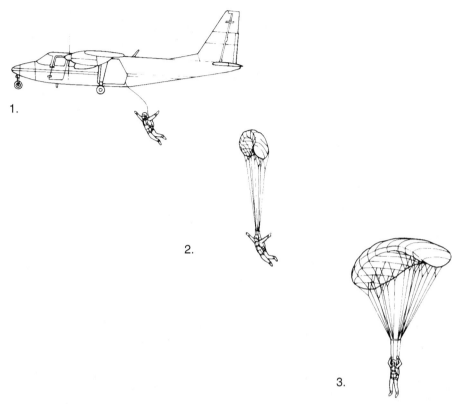

1.

2.

3.

*Static-line
deployment: 1,
the static line
opens the con-
tainer; 2, the
canopy leaves
the bag; 3, full
inflation.*

*A static-line
class under
instruction.*

group is present, there are generally several instructors on hand to ensure that a student who does not grasp things straight away is given the personal attention that they need.

After their first jump has been debriefed and critiqued, the novice now has the choice to continue in the sport along a progression system that will take them to free fall and eventually to one of the experienced disciplines we will examine later.

The static line/free fall progression programme is popular because it enables the novice to experience the sport without having to make a large time or financial commitment. It is accessible to most income brackets and, because subsequent jumps are paid for individually, and most progression training is generally free, means that the customer can control the amount that they spend. In the next chapter, we will take a detailed look at the skills that must be learned in order to make a first jump safely on this system. First, however, a couple of alternatives.

THE ACCELERATED FREE FALL SYSTEM (AFF)

For many years, the static line programme was the only way to introduce a potential skydiver to our sport. It was considered unwise for a novice to be exposed to free fall

A group of novice static-line students are briefed prior to emplaning.

on their first jump for the following reasons:

- Could they think themselves through the 'sensory overload' that initially accompanies the first few seconds after exit?

- Could they keep their wits about them and orientate their bodies on a fast airflow so that they had a chance of exerting some control over their environment?

- Could they be guaranteed to provide a stable platform for their canopy's deployment?

- In the drama of the moment, with all the distractions present, could they be relied upon to pull the ripcord at all?

For a long time, the answer to these questions was considered to be 'No'. Even though, in wartime, many pilots and aircrew had bailed out of stricken aircraft with primitive parachute systems and managed to save their lives by pulling a ripcord, few of these heroic individuals would admit to being totally in control of their situation.

In the late 1970s however, in the USA, a new form of skydiving instruction was developed. At this time, around the world, the standard of instruction and free-fall ability amongst instructors and coaches was improving rapidly. Experienced parachutists were doing more jumps, and using them constructively to amass free-fall time and push the limits of what could be achieved in terms of formation skydiving. If we consider that an average skydive from 12,000–13,000ft (3,500–3,800m) gives someone about a minute in free fall, and then consider the amount of time that a rock climber or squash player spends practising their sport each time they participate, we can see that skill and true experience in free fall takes a long while and many

jumps to accumulate.

Accelerated Free Fall (AFF) teaching came into being. It is sometimes assumed that this means one actually goes faster in free fall! This is not the case, the 'accelerated' part of the name refers to the speed at which free-fall skills are learned.

After an intensive course lasting, again, one or two days, the novice is taken to altitude by two AFF instructors. The student wears a rig similar to that of the static-line novice, but it is a true free-fall system equipped with a ripcord and pilot chute that they must eventually operate themselves. At altitude, the student will be launched from the aircraft door by the two instructors who will have taken jumpsuit or harness grips on either side of them. Over the next sixty or seventy seconds, as the student reacts to their training and attempts to relax and control themselves on the fast airflow, the instructors are continuously present to help and give input to them.

The two most apparent advantages of this system are that the student gains experience of their environment in increments of one minute, instead of a few seconds, each jump, and also that any corrective instruction to correct body position and so on can be given there and then, as the mistakes occur. This corrective input is given via a series of hand signals that can be brought to the student's attention at any time during the skydive. As we will see later, these signals can be used not just to correct body position, but to help the student become aware of their altitude and to instruct or remind them to pull at the correct altitude. Should the student lose awareness for any reason, the AFF instructors are on hand to initiate the pull for them.

Having successfully completed their first jump, or 'Level One', the novice is progressed over a series of seven levels, during which time they amass the free-fall skills and awareness that will be required of them as an intermediate skydiver. The idea is that they take fewer jumps to reach this standard than someone progressing on the conventional progression system. This is certainly true to a great extent, although it can be argued that they gain these skills at a more superficial level and that because they will have less jumps than a conventional student, they do not have the same basic feel for the air at an intermediate level. Some national bodies, including the BPA, insist that an AFF student makes a further ten 'consolidation' jumps upon graduation, in order to revise their skills in more depth.

The truth is that both the AFF system and the more conventional static line/free fall progression method are equally effective. Both have produced world-class skydivers. They should be considered as two roads that climb the same mountain, reaching the top by different routes, but ultimately achieving the same objective. An AFF course is necessarily more expensive, whether a student pays for all eight levels at the outset of their training or chooses to pay level-by-level. The instruction is done on a very personalized basis and is very labour intensive from the instructor's point of view. Each skydive must be practised repeatedly on the ground and must be debriefed in detail if the novice is to progress safely and learn from their mistakes.

On both progression systems, a student can be progressed after each jump or asked to repeat a particular skill on a subsequent jump. This 'repeat' option is available to the instructor who is ultimately responsible for allowing a student to progress quickly, but at a rate that is right for them.

Both the options detailed above are designed to train someone to skydive. The courses form part of a structured progression system, and though they are used by many as the means to make their one and only jump, there are those who feel they would like to experience the thrill of free fall and the gentle exhilaration of a ram-air canopy ride without the responsibility or trouble of training for it. There are also those who prefer to spend their hard-earned leisure time dipping in and out of various adventure sports. Until recent years, these individuals could not be accommodated by our sport. There was simply no way of getting them airborne without undergoing an involved training programme. Now that has all changed: since its inception in the early 1980s and subsequent adoption around the world, there is now a method of introducing individuals to skydiving with minimum training and time investment. It's the ultimate fairground ride...

TANDEM SKYDIVING (THE QUICK FIX!)

The concept of tandem skydiving is simple. Just about every form of transport known to man has the facility to take passengers, and now this applies to skydiving as well. Using a specially developed parachute system containing two very large ram-air canopies (main and reserve) and a passenger harness, a tandem instructor can take a novice to altitude after the briefest period of instruction. They can dive from the aircraft door as one unit and experience a lengthy free fall with the instructor (effectively riding piggyback on the passenger) exerting complete control. At the correct altitude, the instructor can initiate parachute deployment in the normal way, and the two can make an extended canopy ride to the ground, landing the canopy by flaring as normal.

The equipment used for tandem skydiv-

Tandem free fall; note the drogue bridle towing behind.

ing is not simply a scaled-up version of a personal skydiving rig. It has several features that directly address the particular needs of this discipline. The passenger harness is more or less the same as any parachute harness except that it attaches to the canopies and rig via the instructor. Two steel snap hooks on the passenger's shoulders are connected and safety locked to a point below the three-ring release on the instructor's harness. Two further snap hooks attach at waist height past the instructor to the main container. These are generally adjusted loosely for the climb to altitude so that both parties have some independent movement. They are, however, pulled very tight for exit and free fall so that the instructor is effectively 'sandwiched' between passenger and rig. Once out of the aircraft, it is imperative that the passenger

can make no independent movement or 'washing about' relative to the instructor: this could make control in free fall very difficult.

The tandem system is also fitted with a large drogue parachute that is deployed shortly after exit. Instead of immediately opening the main canopy, this will inflate and tow behind the pair. Having twice the mass but the same effective surface area of a single skydiver means that the tandem pair would accelerate and fall at about 180mph (290km/h) instead of the normal 120mph (190km/h). This would make for a very hard opening that would possibly damage both skydivers and equipment. The drogue prevents this excessive speed. A by-product of the 'drogue fall' is that single skydivers can fly quite happily with the tandem pair. Most drop zones offer the opportunity

Tandem dive exit.

Packing the tandem drogue.

for a tandem passenger to have their own personal video person to record the event from briefing, through the aircraft ride and free fall, to the canopy ride and landing. This is only possible because a mutual fall rate can be achieved.

The tandem instructor will generally open the main canopy at about 5,000ft (1,500m). This is higher than normal to allow a safe margin for any deployment problems that may occur. It also permits an extended canopy ride. A ripcord is pulled that simultaneously releases and collapses the drogue, allowing it to act as a normal

Tandem opening.

*Tandem
landing.*

pilot chute and open the canopy in about four seconds. Once in control of the parachute, the instructor will loosen off the side adjusters and usually hand a pair of dual control steering toggles to the passenger, who will help to fly the canopy down to the landing area. Because of the immense size of a tandem main canopy, usually in excess of 400sq ft (37sq m), it can be landed just as softly as a personal parachute, with the flare being made in the normal way.

The complete lack of fear exhibited by most tandem passengers is startling! Bearing in mind that they sometimes only meet the instructor ten minutes or so before boarding the aircraft, the willingness to surrender all their imagined safety to a stranger has always surprised me. I think that it has something to do with the absence of any formal instruction. Sometimes conventional parachute students are more scared of their inability to perform under stress than they are of the environment. If you remove the responsibility to make decisions, as is the case with a tandem student, then most of the reason for the fear is removed also.

Any form of instructor is continually reminded of their own first jump through the reactions of their students. With tandem, this reaction is immediate. Sometimes a tandem student is literally rendered speechless by the free fall they have experienced; conversely, others cannot be silenced for several hours after the experience!

The final manner in which tandem differs from other skydiving disciplines is that it allows people to experience our sport who, because of health problems or previous injury, would not be allowed to participate. Although instructors and centres must always display a responsible attitude to the passengers that they accept, parachuting and skydiving are now available for visually and aurally handicapped people, along with those who have lost limbs or whose condition would normally make the sport inaccessible. Medical advice is always taken in cases such as these.

A large proportion of tandem students are so impressed with the experience that they decide to take a course and become skydivers themselves. Some AFF progression systems offer a tandem jump as a precursor to the AFF course, and some are using it as part of the course itself.

These, then, are the methods used to train skydivers and introduce people to the sport. Having made the decision to participate, let us now look at the training involved to make that all-important first jump.

5 The Initial Training

Before anyone can make a first jump by themselves, there are a number of skills that must be learned to ensure that the student can cope in any situation. These skills apply to AFF as well as to the conventional static-line course, although with the former, a level one skydive will take the place of the first few seconds out of the aircraft door as the static line opens the main canopy.

However the individual subjects are taught, the skills basically divide into two groups:

- Sport skills
- Survival skills

Sport skills deal with the routine sequence of any skydive or parachute descent, the things that *will* happen. These will include, as we shall see, the procedures within the aircraft, the exit, the canopy ride and the landing. Survival skills deal with contingencies, events that we do not expect to routinely happen, but must anticipate. These include malfunctions of the main canopy, aircraft engine failure, and hazard avoidance under canopy. Any student must be taught how unlikely it is for a serious problem to occur, but they must be mentally and physically prepared to deal with it if it does.

Let's examine the formal lessons in the approximate order that they will be taught. Although there will be a general format for each subject, it must be noted that the CCI of any individual centre can choose to put the information across however they wish. The lesson content listed here is the way that I teach, and should not be regarded as hard and fast. Some centres will train a basic course in one day; some will spread it over two.

ORIENTATION

This is a general familiarization session. The instructor will meet their students in a classroom environment and appraise them of the format for the day's training. They will be shown the airfield and any particular hazards that relate to them. They will also be briefed on any documentation that they have completed and the general rules of parachuting as they apply to their course.

The orientation lesson also gives the instructor the opportunity to get to know their students. A mutual respect and trust needs to be built up throughout the course, and it starts in this lesson. Any good teacher uses their personality to the full as they impart information, and an instructor that gets the class on their side from the start will not only have an easier job, but produce a better product in terms of quality of parachutist.

The fun aspect of the sport must be stressed to the full. As we have previously stated, that is the only reason for anyone to come skydiving!

EQUIPMENT FAMILIARIZATION

A thorough introduction to the equipment now follows. In addition to the handling and function of each item, a general sense of confidence and security must prevail. The container system and canopies have been thoroughly tested over many thousands of jumps, and are loaded to many times the force to which they will be exposed. A student must be made aware of this.

Personal equipment is also introduced at this stage. A jumpsuit is worn that will provide a consistent surface for the parachute harness and prevent the clothing underneath obscuring any ripcord handles at embarrassing moments! It is a good idea to have students wearing jumpsuits throughout the course: not only does it keep them warm, but it helps to establish a sense of 'team' and identity. The jumpsuits must contrast in colour to the emergency handles on the front of the rig.

Most schools will provide their students with an altimeter and radio. The radio enables a ground operator to assist with canopy control, although the students must be taught to think for themselves and the radio considered as very much a back-up device. The altimeter must also be explained. Traditionally used as a guide in free fall, the visual altimeter is an essential tool to the student parachutist, who has little idea initially of what the ground looks like from various heights. Altimeters react to change of atmospheric pressure, and this pressure lessens the further one rises above sea level. The altimeter, therefore, will have a calibration dial so that it can be zeroed before each jump to cope with local changes in pressure caused by the weather. As we will see, student canopy control is best expressed as a series of appointments at various altitudes over certain features on the ground.

All students are required to wear a helmet of sorts. Although there is little danger

Examining the open canopy.

of their head striking anything in the normal course of events, it is mandatory to wear one as a precautionary measure.

The parachute equipment will then be explained in as much detail as we have seen in Chapter 3. This session will invariably include a fitting of the gear also. There are three main points of adjustment on a normal parachute harness: one sliding friction lock adjuster on each leg strap, and one on the chest strap. This enables the rig to be adjusted to fit just about anybody. Centres will usually stock smaller harnesses for the shorter student. A harness needs to fit comfortably and evenly, which means tight but not restrictive. It should move with the parachutist's body without moving relative to it, and be snug enough so that there is no secondary shock from the opening. These days parachute systems are simple enough so that most students can be left to fit their own, but all students must receive a thorough equipment check by an instructor prior to enplaning. It must be impossible for them to enter the aircraft with any self-generated error.

In addition to the equipment features we have already examined, there are two further features that are common to most student parachute systems these days. They are further safety back-up systems and, although they are optional extras for experienced skydivers, are becoming regarded as essential for all students under our care.

The Reserve Static Line (RSL)

This feature consists of a shackle or connector link that attaches to one riser of the main parachute and is connected by a tape lanyard to a ring around the reserve ripcord cable, secured some distance above the pin. If the main is jettisoned in the event of a malfunction – a cutaway – the main canopy will therefore force the reserve ripcord pin

to be pulled as it flies away from the jumper. In effect, this makes it possible for the student to perform only one action in a stress situation instead of two. A student must, however, always be taught to pull the reserve ripcord manually whether the RSL has performed or not. The responsibility for a successful reserve deployment ultimately rests with the individual.

The Automatic Activation Device (AAD)

These systems have been around the skydiving world for over twenty years, but it is only recently that they have appeared in electronic form, increasing their reliability and accuracy.

The AAD will be calibrated at ground level prior to the start of the day's jumping. From that time on, it will continuously compare the ambient air pressure with a rate of ascent (in the aircraft), or a rate of descent (in free fall or under canopy). In short, if the jumper's rate of descent is far too great as they pass through a given altitude, then the AAD will activate. Depending on the model, it will either pull the reserve ripcord, or cut or burn through the closure loop. This will, of course, initiate the reserve opening. It is very reassuring for a student to learn of this device, and good for the instructor for them to have that confidence, but only if that knowledge is tempered with the realization that this, once more, is a back-up device that does not substitute for a good manual reserve drill.

THE STABLE POSITION

Having gained some confidence in their equipment, the student then learns how to use it. The stable position is the cornerstone of the art of free fall, and more than any other part of the course, a springboard for further progression.

No matter what a skydiver achieves in free fall, no matter what manoeuvres they attempt in terms of turns, back loops or formation building, they will always return to a standard face-to-earth position for the pull. Because the canopies are located on their back, this must be uppermost for a clean deployment.

On the AFF program, this position will be practised throughout the skydive with two instructors remaining hands-on. For a first jump on the static-line system, the student is on their own, and must hold this position for about five to six seconds as the canopy deploys.

The principle of stability is simple. A spread shape is adopted, with the arms at shoulder level and slightly bent. The legs are almost straight and slightly more than shoulder width apart. If the head is held straight, a symmetrical position results. Symmetry is important because if the airflow hits an uneven shape, a turn will result that is not commensurate with a clean opening or controlled free fall.

The other component of the position is even more important: the arch. A spread position by itself shows a flat section to the air. This means that the air must buffet the jumper in free fall: it must move them out of the way in order to flow past them. If the skydiver bends back from their waist and presents a smooth arch, they are effectively stable on their column of air, and their passage through it is smooth. The shape and balance of a shuttlecock is a very accurate analogy.

The student is taught to assume this

The stable position from the front. Note the symmetry.

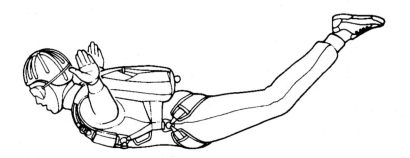

The stable position from the side showing a good arch.

The stable position in the air – very good throughout, excellent arch.

Practising the stable position on the ground.

position as they perform the release from the aircraft, so that the first shape that the air sees is the correct one. Usually preceded by a loud 'GO!' from the jumpmaster, the exit must be forceful and smooth. During training, the technique should be practised repeatedly, with corrective input given where necessary. What the instructor needs is a semi-conditioned response to their command so that the drama of the situation, the fast air and the disorientation, will be over-ridden. For most students, the first few seconds out of the door is the most enjoyable, and scary, part of their first jump.

There tend to be certain 'standard' mistakes made by students during these first few seconds. These will be identified by the jumpmaster at the post-jump debrief in order that the student will learn to correct them on subsequent skydives. The debrief is as important as the actual jump itself for any progressing student, whatever system they are on. Video is used extensively these days, particularly on later free falls, so that a novice can see for themself errors in position and understand exactly what they did. Among the most common 'standard' mistakes are:

- **Looking down flat position** With the head forced back on release from the aircraft, a good arch is almost guaranteed. It is, however, instinctive to glance at the ground as you leave. This will flatten the body position and make it hard for the air to hold you stable: a turn or roll will result.

- **Legs kicking** Possibly for the first time ever, the novice has nothing to brace their feet against. A common reaction, again instinctive, is to move the legs or kick. This again results in a bad position which can roll you on to your back.

- **De-arched, rolling unstable** Sometimes, in the heat of the moment, a student will bend forward at the waist on release. This has the effect of trying to lie on top of a large beach ball! Invariably you will roll off the top and instability will result.

Remember that on AFF severely bad body positions are rare because of the direct instructor control. Also, with the standard of instruction such as it is these days, it is rare for a static-line student to lose control completely. Even in that event, modern equipment is designed to cope to a large extent with bad body position. Bear in mind also

Looking down – slightly de-arched.

that, because of the static line, the main parachute is deploying from the first second anyway, and will soon pull the student upright regardless of what their body is doing. None of this, however, detracts from the fact that a stable exit is important.

On the conventional progression system, a 'safety count' is also taught. On release from the aircraft, as they burst into position, a student will also begin to count. It is important that every skydiver gives sufficient time for their canopy to deploy before they look up to check it, but not too long. An experienced jumper will normally perform a mental four second count. However, with a student, overloaded as they are likely to be, this process has to be loud and positive. The count must cut through the fear and drama. It is even more important than the body position.

'1,000, 2,000, 3,000, 4,000, 5,000, 6,000, CHECK CANOPY!'

The precise duration of the count varies from centre to centre. With a ram-air canopy, I prefer a slightly longer count than the traditional four-second one. Ram-airs open progressively and if a student counts too fast (very common) it is possible they could mistake the final stages of deployment for a problem.

AIRCRAFT DRILLS

As we have seen, the aircraft ride is a necessary part of any jump. Students must be taught what to expect during the climb to altitude. It is surprisingly common for people who have never flown before, even

Weak release – de-arch, going unstable.

commercially, to attend skydiving courses! Therefore, this part of the experience is sometimes as much a test of their nerves as everything else. Even those who have flown regularly will not have done so in a light aircraft rigged for skydiving with the door removed!

The types of aircraft used for parachuting around the world vary enormously. At large commercial centres it is not uncommon to use two or more: often a large fast turbine-engined aircraft with a big lift capacity for experienced jumpers who want a warm, fast ride to high altitude and a smaller, possibly piston-engined, aircraft to handle the student operation. Any aircraft used for students must be equipped with a strongpoint (for static line attachment) and must be able to fly slowly enough for the canopies to deploy in a reasonable airflow. Smaller centres will generally just have one aircraft that all jumpers will share.

Students will be taught the sequence of events that will take them from the 'flight-line', where equipment checks are made and final briefings are given, to the aircraft itself and the subsequent take-off. They must be taught the danger of moving propellers, and to approach the aircraft from the rear. They will have allotted seating positions that give each student access to the jump door when required. They will also be taught to protect their emergency handles and move on command only. This is so that the instructor can keep control of any movement and be on hand to deal with any situation as it occurs. Aircraft equipped for parachuting have as much of the interior removed as possible. Seats, seatbelt mountings, surplus control columns and so on will all have been removed and stored to provide as much room as possible. Space is always at a premium.

Once again, precise procedures vary from place to place, but the instructor is always positioned by the door. This ensures that he/she is always in a position to give control as necessary as students make their exits. Static-line control is also critical at this time. The line that will open the student's canopy needs to have a clear run from the strongpoint, through the instructor's hands, to the closure pin on the student's back.

The exit and release from the aircraft should be practised repeatedly on the ground and, once again, mistakes corrected immediately. It is a simple procedure to move your body from a position inside the aircraft, to one poised on the edge of the door; however, it is a little different when everything is suddenly real and there is 3,500ft (1,000km/h) of clear air below you and a 75mph (120km/h) slipstream to contend with. Once again, training must be deep, it must dominate and overcome the natural fear that accompanies any first jump. It is a credit to the standard of instruction practised around the world these days that most students make a real good job of this part of their skydive.

On an AFF jump, the student and instructors leave the aircraft as one unit. As the primary and secondary instructors have harness or jumpsuit grips on the student, they can dominate the situation immediately and give what input is necessary to correct body position. This exit will lead into the level one skydive that we will look at in detail later in this chapter.

AIRCRAFT EMERGENCIES

Every parachutist must be taught of the potential problems that can occur during a flight. Some of these are common to all powered aviation and some are peculiar to parachuting. We can separate them into three distinct categories.

Practising the exit.

Aircraft Problems

These can include engine failure, loss of control and fire – situations that can happen in any aircraft, at any time. In the rare event of any of these happening, the parachutist has one obvious advantage over conventional passengers – they can get out and leave the problem behind! Given that the pilot is ultimately in command, quick decisive liaison with the jumpmaster is essential. The decision to jump or stay with the aircraft will be based on several factors.

- **What altitude is the aircraft at?** In an emergency situation, any parachutist will be expected to jump at a lower altitude than normal. If the alternative is a fatal crash, normal safety margins cease to apply.

- **What level of experience is on board?** If the parachutists are seasoned, experienced skydivers, the jumpmaster will probably be hard pushed to prevent them leaving! If, however, they are first-jump students, the jumpmaster will have to consider their state of mind and the

In the classroom.

possibility that they will be slow or reluctant to move. It is impossible to make hard-and-fast rules based on altitude, as every situation is unique and demands a spur of the moment decision.

- **What ground is the aircraft flying over?** An instructor with students on board may make a different decision if there are power lines and a main road directly below the aircraft rather than clear, open fields. Parachute pilots do not habitually fly over built-up areas, but unless the drop zone is in a desert, it is sometimes unavoidable.

If the decision is taken to make a forced landing with the aircraft, all jumpers must be braced for the touchdown and moved as far forward as possible to prevent secondary movement as it comes to a sudden stop. Bear in mind that part of the reason that we wear helmets is to protect us in such an event.

As soon as the aircraft has stopped, whether there is fire or not, all jumpers must leave quickly and without panic. If static-line students are involved, this may involve the instructor cutting the static line with a knife to avoid wasting time by unhooking everyone.

Premature Deployment

The second potential aircraft problem involves the parachutes themselves. If either a main or reserve canopy is allowed to deploy inside the aircraft while it is in flight, everyone on board is in serious danger. If the deploying canopy is allowed to exit the aircraft while the wearer is still on board, they will be instantly and violently pulled towards the door. The forces involved are such that as they collide with the rear doorframe they will probably damage the

aircraft and receive fatal injuries themselves.

It is obviously imperative that this situation is not allowed to happen. Student parachutists are taught to move only on command from the instructor, and to protect their ripcord handles at all times. Experienced jumpers are responsible for making sure that their equipment is as secure as it needs to be to prevent the situation from arising. Any premature deployment must be controlled and contained immediately, and the aircraft brought to the ground as soon as possible.

Static-Line Hang-Up

As the name suggests, this emergency is peculiar to static-line parachuting. It is at the same time the least common and most easily preventable of all parachuting emergencies. We have previously seen how the static line pulls the deployment bag from its container as the student falls away. If for any reason the line becomes fouled with the jumper, or has been allowed to pass through some part of their equipment, the possibility exists that it will lock, and leave the stunned and bewildered student hanging underneath the aircraft door – hence the name. Control at all times is the watchword for prevention. Control during the packing process, discipline on the flight line when the students are given their static lines to hold, and careful movement inside the aircraft and during the exit. The instructor must be in complete control of the static line before they give the command to go. They will ensure that the line has a clear run to the back of the container and is not allowed to interfere with any part of the student's body. The student plays their part by responding to commands as they are given and not applying creative thought to moving around the cabin or into the door!

If a hang-up ever does occur, there is a fairly standard procedure for dealing with it. Given that it will probably happen during the first second after exit, the student will become immediately aware that something is drastically wrong. The huge jolt and absence of any canopy will provide a large clue, backed up by the fact that the aircraft is still very close and remaining there. Probably taking a few seconds to react, they will place both their hands on their head. This will show the instructor that they are conscious and aware of the situation, that their upper limbs are unbroken, and that they are not immediately going to panic and start pulling handles. The instructor will now take the aircraft knife and attempt to show it to the student. Whether they can see it or not, the static line will be severed very shortly afterwards. There is no possibility of rectifying a hang-up in any other way. The parachutist cannot be pulled back inside, and the aircraft can obviously not be landed with them still in place. As the static line is cut, any chance of the main canopy deploying has gone, and reserve procedures must be carried out straight away.

It is at this point on a parachute course that the jaws tend to drop! Instructors, however, will provide reassurance by teaching the drills necessary for the prevention of this particular aircraft emergency.

A final point to bear in mind is that the majority of skydivers enjoy the sport over a period of many years without ever encountering any of the above situations. Due to teaching methods and time-honoured procedures they are extremely rare.

CANOPY CONTROL

As the main canopy develops above the student, whether from the static line or an AFF ripcord pull, they now enter the more lengthy and sedate portion of their first jump. For the remainder of the descent to be successful, and result in an accurate, safe landing, they will have been taught the basics of ram-air canopy control.

All canopy control starts from a predetermined opening point. This will have been selected at the start of the day, usually in the following manner. A wind drift indicator (WDI) is dropped from the jump aircraft directly over the desired landing area. This is a tight roll of crêpe paper, weighted slightly at one end of the roll. The WDI quickly unrolls and becomes a brightly coloured streamer that descends towards the ground. It is easily visible from the aircraft or the ground. Usually dropped from about 2,000ft (600m), it will take just under two minutes to reach the ground, and will have drifted in a straight line downwind of the target.

The jumpmaster will take the imaginary line (wind-line) and project it upwind of the target. The students' opening point will be along this line. The stronger the wind, the further the WDI will have travelled, consequently the opening point will be further upwind. Usually, the opening point is about twice the distance of the WDI, upwind of the target. This procedure sounds very primitive, but has proved its accuracy for students over many years.

Now we have a starting point for our canopy control. The student knows that whatever else happens, at least they started from an ideal place, with the wind attempting to blow them back towards the target.

As soon as the main canopy is open, a series of checks is performed:

1. **Check Canopy** Is the canopy fully inflated? Is it malfunctioning in any way and is it flying on heading? This is the

Canopy control lesson.

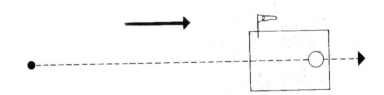

Opening point showing the wind line to target; the arrow indicates wind direction.

single most important action that a student will make.

2. **Check Airspace** Are there any other canopies bearing down on you, or even close? Most centres despatch students one on each pass over the airfield, so there is unlikely to be anyone near. However, in an AFF scenario, or on a student's

later progression, this becomes a possibility. With the high closing speeds of modern canopies, awareness should be maintained throughout the descent.

3. **Check Handles** Are your emergency handles still in their Velcro pockets? With well maintained equipment, it is hard to dislodge them accidentally, but remem-

ber that the exit is a dramatic time, and a reserve handle that is hanging loosely is a hazard.

These checks are done as soon as possible after the canopy opens, in order for maximum time to be spent flying around and simply having fun.

In years past, when parachutes were considerably less mobile, canopy control was simply a matter of making your way down a wind-line towards the target. These days, because of the increased forward speed of most student canopies, the whole procedure is spread out into three dimensions.

Understandably, the average student will take a few seconds to calm down after their first exit, but as quickly as possible they should locate the intended target area, as

all canopy control relates to this. Because canopies and students can turn on exit, the target can be anywhere around them. They may have to make a turn to find it. We have seen that there are different types of turn possible on a ram-air, but for the initial jumps the student will probably just pull one toggle all the way down until they are facing in the intended direction. This simplifies things in a situation where information 'overload' is possible.

A 'holding area' will have been pre-determined. This is an area of land over which they will spend most of their time under canopy. Typically it will straddle the wind-line some distance upwind of the target. As long as they stay within this area at the correct height, they will always have the potential to make it back home.

Examining the canopy.

Working out a landing approach.

The wind speed is a big consideration. If the upper winds are high, the ground speed of the canopy will vary tremendously depending on which way it is faced. If a canopy is facing downwind ('running'), the wind speed is added to the airspeed, and the ground speed increases. If the canopy is faced into wind ('holding'), the airspeed counters the wind speed to some extent and the ground speed decreases. It is easy to confuse a student during canopy control training. Ultimately it is not important that they remember the particular words that we use to describe things, only that they realize some basic truths:

- The canopy will try to move in whichever direction it is faced.

- It will move faster when it is faced downwind.

During their time within the holding area, students are free to have fun and experiment. They will want to practise some turns, and probably some simulated landing flares. It is a good idea that they get a feel for the flare and what it feels like to

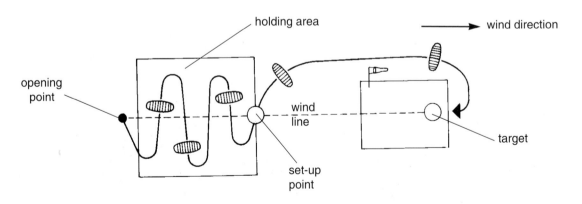

Holding area, possible set-up point and target approach superimposed on the wind line.

Surfing down the slipstream.

Formation with a bemused tandem student.

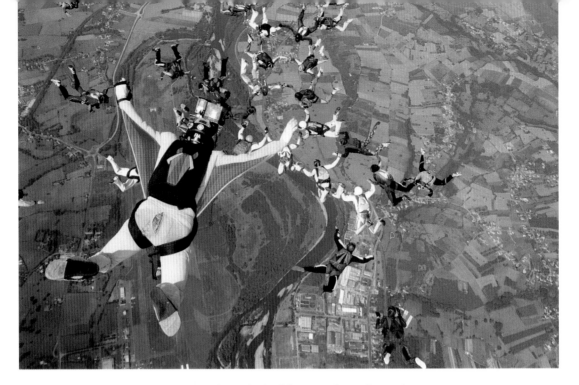

A camera jumper uses wings to stay above the build-up to a large formation.

Head down at 10,000ft towards a thin layer of cloud.

...way diamond completes over the Peterborough
...hute Centre.

...ng the sunset and friends.

Freefly exit at 13,000ft on a summer's day.

Build-up to a large sit-fly formation.

Over the edge ...

A large CRW stack.

The camera is in amongst the action during a hectic Skyvan exit.

Formation skydiving.

Skydiving can improve your looks!

Eye contact throughout as a formation prepares to transition.

Early morning sun on the drop zone as canopies collect after the first load.

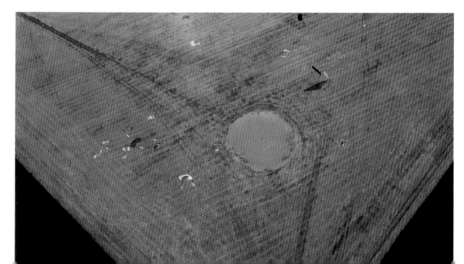

Tailgate exit.

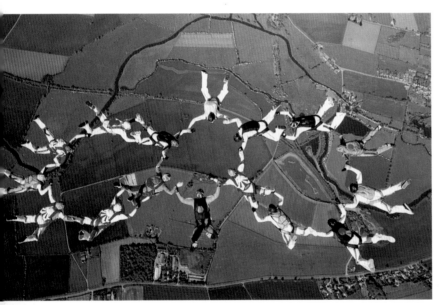

Perfect symmetry.

If anyone asks you why we skydive, show them this.

Some tandem passengers keep their eyes open ...

... some choose not to!

A tandem pair surfing on a thin cloud layer.

Student canopy on final approach – into wind, toggles up.

It is a good idea that the student checks their altimeter and location between manoeuvres. This will prevent any straying from the holding area.

As their descent progresses, they will have been taught to approach a set-up point. This is defined as a small patch of land on the downwind side of their holding area. It will be a good point at which to begin their eventual landing approach. Generally, 1,500ft (450m) is a good height to arrive here. By now, the student is closer to the drop zone and can clearly see any markers that have been laid out to help them. There will invariably be a windsock at the intended target. This is a constant readout of the wind direction and is invaluable to student and experienced jumpers alike.

Because the canopy must be landed facing into wind to reduce ground speed, at some stage before their final approach, a circuit must be flown that takes the jumper downwind of, and past, the target so that they may turn back. How far they fly past on a particular day is governed by the wind speed. If the wind is strong and they fly too far past, they will never make it back. Consequently, if the wind is very light, they will want to travel quite some distance downwind because, when they turn back, their ground speed will be high, and some small turns may be necessary to prevent an overshoot.

Remember that all student landing areas are large. This gives a built-in margin for error. It is more important that a novice jumper lands in a safe area and correctly, rather than become 'target-fixated'.

Finally, the landing. Although students are taught to judge the correct flaring height for themselves, it is now that the radio is used to best effect. A skilled operator will have no trouble talking novices into perfect landings every time. The hardest thing from the parachutist's perspective is

'borrow' lift. Student canopies are de-tuned, so they cannot be made to stall. Usually the ground radio operator, after making initial contact, will leave the student pretty much to their own devices at this time. It is important that their experience is not spoiled by a continuous transmission that can detract from that experience and take away the student's decision-making ability.

leaving the flare late enough. Traditionally, students tend to flare a little high if left to their own devices. On low wind days, when the forward speed of the canopy is most apparent, this is exaggerated, as the student equates forward speed with ground proximity.

In the event of a high flare, the canopy will round out and gently go into a sink. The student's instinct at this time is to let both toggles up and try again. If they do this, the canopy will surge and dive them into the ground. A better alternative is to keep the toggles down and let the canopy sink. The descent rate will certainly increase slightly, but a well-executed parachute roll (*see* below) will allow the jumper to escape without incident.

Canopy control is a skill that can only be partially learned in the classroom. There is no substitute for jumping again and again in different conditions and learning from any previous errors. Although pretty much alone in the sky at the moment, the novice is being readied for the time when they will jump faster canopies, in higher winds, and with many other canopies in the air.

A safe landing in their correct area is the perfect end to a first jump. It adds to the sense of achievement gained by the whole experience. Above all it demonstrates to the student, and to the public at large, that what we teach actually works.

Hazardous landings are usually taught alongside the canopy control lesson. These are survival skills that will enable a novice parachutist – preferably – to avoid a hazard, but if necessary to land on it in such a way that they minimize any injury.

PARACHUTE LANDING FALLS (PLFs)

This is one skill that has been taught to all parachutists since the inception of the sport, and to all military parachutists before that. It is the most basic of all safety skills.

With the advent of student ram-air canopies, and the resultant soft, stand-up landings, it is tempting to sideline PLFs, as the skill itself takes time to learn correctly and most students go through their

Parachute landing falls.

progression without having to resort to using it. However, in the event of a fast downwind landing, or a landing in a tree or similar hazard, it is essential that the parachutist knows how to protect their body in the best way possible.

On round canopies there is a constant descent rate, and so a military parachutist or a sport student using them will use a PLF routinely on every jump.

To achieve the basic position the student, staying vertical in the harness, will:

- Force both feet and knees tightly together.

- Bend slightly at the knees, keeping the flat of the feet presented to the ground.

- Raise the arms above the head and turn the elbows in (unless a flared landing is being made).

- Force the chin down onto the chest.

At the moment of contact, the jumper's weight will be spread over the base of the feet, and the knees will give to protect the spine from jarring. Each leg will splint the other and stay as a tight unit that will prevent separation and buckling.

The other factor is horizontal movement over the ground. As the jumper strikes the ground, they will start to fall in the direction of travel. If they have previously turned off their feet to present a side of the leg, then the knees will be protected. The jumper will now lean their shoulder away from the direction of fall and roll down the curved side of the body. As they fall, they will turn the shoulder away and encourage the roll to travel over their back, coming to rest on the other side. Trust me. It's easier to perform than to describe.

On ram-air canopy courses, the PLF

is taught as a survival skill to enable the jumper to cope with an abnormal landing.

MALFUNCTIONS AND RESERVE DRILLS

This is generally the final new subject to be taught. It is purely a survival skill, nothing to do with fun and enjoyment at all. Teaching must balance confidence in equipment with the realization that these emergency situations are rare, but realistic. In skydiving terms, a malfunction is defined as a canopy that has failed to deploy correctly within its given timescale. As the years have progressed, malfunctions have become less and less common. Equipment is now manufactured to higher standards, packing procedures have become refined, and the ability of the average skydiver is such that they can do everything possible to discourage these situations from happening.

Throughout the course, a student has been bombarded with images of a properly formed main canopy. By the time they enter this period of instruction, they will have this image to use as a template against which to compare less favourable images. There are four main types of malfunction:

Total

The main canopy has completely failed to deploy. At the end of their safety count, the student finds themself in free fall. On the static line, this could only happen if the line was not connected to the aircraft. In the case of a free-fall student, it could occur if they had experienced a very stiff pull, or could not locate the handle.

Recognition – There is no canopy visible

Suspended harness work.

whatsoever, and instead of being suspended in a calm environment, the jumper is still exposed to the drama of free fall.

Why it won't happen – The instructor will connect the static line, and the student will double check this visually.

Solution – Cutaway and deploy reserve.

Streamer

The canopy has emerged from the deployment bag and pulled the student mostly upright, but deployment has halted at this stage and no inflation has occurred. If the lines are knotted below the slider, or it is held under the canopy for some reason, the canopy, although otherwise fine, will not open.

Recognition – The canopy appears small and is probably flapping dramatically instead of being large and solid. There is wind noise and drama.

Why it won't happen – Correct packing will ensure that the lines release in stows and cannot knot or bundle. The student will perform a good exit to encourage this.

Solution – Cutaway and deploy reserve.

Line-Over

The canopy has left the bag and inflated,

but one side has inverted under a line group, and there are lines trapped over it.

Recognition – The canopy is distorted. The airfoil is not intact. Most line-over malfunctions on ram-air canopies involve a rotation of some degree.

Why it won't happen – For the same reasons as the streamer.

Solution – Cutaway and deploy reserve.

Damage

There is damage apparent when the canopy is checked, either to the nylon of the parachute itself or to the suspension lines.

Recognition – There is loose material or broken lines. Obviously the amount of damage will affect the situation. Possibly a rotation will occur simultaneously.

Why it won't happen – The canopy is inspected during the packing process from the previous jump. The canopy and lines are deployed in stages and should never interfere with each other.

Solution – Cutaway and deploy reserve.

Dealing with a Malfunction

The reason that malfunctions are a problem is simple. They all result in a canopy that is descending faster than normal, and cannot be steered effectively. During training, the student must be taught to make a fast, accurate decision from an image presented to them, preferably on video. Obviously from what we have seen, some malfunctions are initially more serious than others. Some schools may teach pupils to attempt to take control of a minor problem, and make a decision by a certain altitude. Others may throw a 'blanket' over all situations and insist on one procedure for all bad situations. Whatever the teaching, it should take account of the likely state of mind of the student at the time of recognition, and the need for as few decisions as possible. In all teaching, simple is best.

I teach one drill to deal with all malfunctions:

Look Once the decision has been made, the cutaway and reserve handles should become the complete focus of attention.

Locate One hand to each handle, grasped as a fist.

Peel, Punch The cutaway pad is peeled from its Velcro and punched aggressively down in line with the body. The student is now falling away from the stricken main canopy.

Peel, Punch The reserve handle is similarly peeled and punched downward. The reserve has now been activated.

Arch The student now reassumes a hard arch position. If they have been thrown unstable by the cutaway, this will not have time to turn them face to earth, but it will clear their limbs away from the body and guard against any possible temptation to grab at the deploying reserve.

The ram-air reserve is now open above the student's head and, a few deep breaths notwithstanding, should be taken control of and flown as normal towards the target.

When practical cutaway and reserve drill are taught, it is essential for students to practise in a suspended harness. As always, realism is best.

NUISANCE FACTORS

There are two nuisance factors associated with ram-air deployment. These are not cutaway situations and are relatively common.

End Cell Closure

Sometimes, when a ram-air inflates, equal pressure is not transmitted throughout all the cells. This can leave the cells on either side appearing limp. Because the canopy has not achieved its full span, the slider can also come to rest a couple of feet above the risers. Simply by releasing the brakes and making two full movements or 'pumps' on the toggles, the angle of attack is changed, allowing the cells to inflate and the slider to complete its journey down the lines.

Line Twists

If the deployment bag turns relative to the jumper during deployment, line twists can be encouraged without adversely affecting the canopy. For a static-line student, an off-heading exit is the most likely cause. The twists serve as a distraction. Provided the main canopy is checked first, the twists can be removed by separating both risers and kicking positively in the right direction.

All student training should be recorded on a log card or log book, and the student issued with the relevant qualification before their first jump. Consequently, they should be critiqued after the jump itself, and sufficient coaching given to correct any errors and to aid them on the road to future progression.

Most people discover a lot about themselves on a sport parachuting course. Many will not have previously placed themselves in pressure situations before, or even in a learning environment of any sort for some years. Most students enjoy the course in its own right, and don't simply view it as a necessary evil on the road to a successful first jump.

6 The Basic Skills

Having successfully made a first jump, and assuming that they have made the decision to continue, the novice is presented with a formal progression system that will take them to an intermediate level. Whether they have trained on a static-line course or made an AFF level one skydive, their next series of jumps will address the skills that are essential to every skydiver.

Progression systems are laid down by the governing body of the sport in a particular country, and therefore differ around the world. The basic skills are the same, however, wherever one jumps, and vary only in the order that they are taught.

THE PULL

All jumpers must eventually initiate a deployment sequence to open their main canopy. The technique for doing this is taught through a series of 'dummy pulls', either on a number of static-line jumps, or during an AFF level one.

From an arched stable position, the right arm is swept back so that the hand can close on the ripcord handle. Because this produces an asymmetrical position, the left hand counters the movement by simultaneously reaching high above the head until it reaches the bodyline. An AFF student will be taught to place the flat of their hand on the handle instead of grasping it. They will usually find their hand guided by the

primary instructor. Someone learning this skill on a static-line jump will actually pull a dummy handle from a pouch.

Instructors will be watching to ensure that the arch is maintained throughout the pull and subsequent recovery. Re-affirming a hard arch as you pull is the best guarantee against losing stability.

An AFF student will normally perform at least two dummy pulls before the real one, and a static-line student at least three consecutive good ones. On the conventional system, this is a very important stage of progression. When they progress to free fall, they are on their own with no guiding hand to assist. It is the instructor's responsibility to make certain that the student can pull confidently, so that the possible psychological barrier of a first free fall is overcome.

FALLING ON A GIVEN HEADING

Having mastered a good stable position, the next stage is to use it on delays of increasing length and faster air. We will look at the AFF progression in detail later, staying for now with the conventional, post-static-line student as they move through the system.

As the length of their delays increases so will the altitude from which they are despatched, in order to achieve a consistent pull height. The longer one falls, the faster the air, and the more that small mistakes in body position will become apparent. After about twelve seconds in a stable fall, the student will reach 'terminal velocity'. This is the fastest that their body mass can achieve in a given position. Up until now, on delays of five or ten seconds, the air has been relatively slow. The object of these early delays is simply to maintain a heading relative to the horizon and pull at the correct height. Time elapsed will be judged by a verbal count that will mark the seconds until the pull. Any trouble that is encountered, such as a rapid turn or instability will be solved by pulling the main ripcord. While small trim problems can be corrected, a student can easily lose track of time if they struggle to sort a major problem. It is a basic tenet of student free fall that pulling a ripcord while unstable or tumbling is preferable to pulling it at a low altitude or not at all.

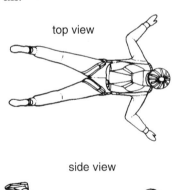

top view

side view

The stable position in a vertical airflow.

Once on fifteen- or twenty-second delays, falling from 5,000–6,000ft (1,500–1,800m), no trim or turn problems should be encountered, providing that a student has not been over-progressed. It is now possible, and beneficial, to relax more. This may not mean changing the basic body position, but simply

taking some of the tension out of it so that it can be more elastic on the air. The natural reaction of anyone in a pressure situation is to 'tense-up' and become rigid. While this an understandable condition in a student free-faller, it is detrimental to true control in free fall. Bear in mind that a hard arch can be held in free fall without the effort or strain of the same position practised on the ground. The airflow exerts a uniform pressure on the falling body, and creates a mould for the skydiver to lie in.

At this stage, the altimeter can be introduced in a free-fall context, whereas it has previously been used solely under canopy. It is impractical and inaccurate to count verbally for more than fifteen seconds: therefore, the altimeter is glanced at periodically throughout the skydive to determine the time left to pull height. The visible dial may be worn on the chest or on the left wrist, where it can be seen without any major change in body position. If an altimeter is watched constantly in free fall, its descent can appear 'jerky', therefore it is better to take 'snapshot' glances of it during the sky-dive.

VERTICAL AXIS TURNS

Once a student has proved their ability to fall on heading in a relaxed position, it is time for them to start working the air properly, and accumulating skills that will be used regularly in later skydives. One of the most basic of these skills is the vertical axis turn.

The turn must be second nature to the experienced jumper because it has so many applications. It will be used to make minor corrections on docking approaches during formation skydiving; it will be used during the transition from one formation to another; and it will always be used at the end of a

Stable delay.

Altimeter check.

formation skydive when jumpers must change heading and move to their own patch of sky in order to open their canopies.

There are many ways to teach and practice a vertical axis body turn, but all involve breaking the body's symmetry in some way in order to deflect air and make the body turn as a reaction to it. I will detail the most commonly taught basic turn.

Once vertical speed has been made, usually about eight or nine seconds after exit, the student will check their altimeter. It is usually sensible rule that the altitude is checked immediately before and after any manoeuvre. The student then looks in the direction they wish to turn, and tilts the upper body down slightly in that direction. The advantage of fast air is to minimize the movement required. If the body is tilted to the right, air will be re-directed to their left, and a right turn will result. The speed of the turn is proportional to the tilt, and it is important at this stage of progression that the manoeuvre does not happen too quickly. As the turn initiates, the jumper is looking ahead of themselves.

If the intention is to make a 360-degree turn, then they will soon see their original heading come into view. If the turn is happening at the correct speed, simply regaining symmetry will cause it to stop. If things are going a little quickly, however, some 'opposite lock' may be required in order to stop accurately on heading. The altimeter is then checked and a decision made as to whether or not to turn again. A student will always be given an 'end of work' altitude to give them sufficient time to pull in an unhurried fashion at the correct altitude. Given an exit altitude of 7,000–8,000ft (2,000–2,500m), and an intended pull at 3,500ft (1,000m), 5,000ft (1,500m) would be a sensible height to finish exercises. If time permits, more turns are a good idea. It is essential to get maximum value from any working jump, as long as safety is not compromised.

As experience grows, the student may be taught to add a leg tilt to their turn, and deflect air from their lower body. This has the advantage of making the turn happen around the true middle of their body. This is necessary during formation skydiving, when the individual needs to remain in place relative to the formation.

The basic body turn to the right. Symmetry is broken and air is deflected to the left.

BACK LOOPS – HORIZONTAL AXIS TURNS

Apart from disciplines such as traditional style or freestyle, the back loop has no practical application at all! It is a manoeuvre made entirely for its own sake – for fun. In some philosophies it is only taught as a way of demonstrating recovery from instability. I believe, however, that a precise on-heading back loop demonstrates a significant

4.

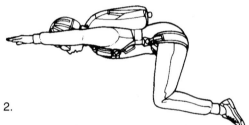

1.

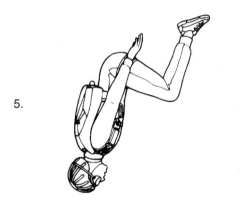

2.

5.

6.

3.

Progression through a backloop.

7.

amount of body control, and therefore is an essential progression exercise.

It differs from the vertical axis turn in that the body position is continually changing throughout the exercise. It is not possible to hold a certain position and do a back loop. It must be flown through, using the pressure of the air as well as momentum to achieve our aim.

Again, speed is achieved and the altimeter checked. Taking note of their ground heading, the student moves their arms *slightly* forward and simultaneously brings both knees up to their chest. This takes air pressure from the lower body and increases it at the top end. The body will then quickly rotate around a horizontal axis passing through the waist. The back loop is now achieved by pushing down with both arms, as though upon two parallel bars. As the legs swing through, the head can be thrown back. A backward somersault results. It is very important to anticipate the end of the back loop, which will come about very quickly. As the legs pass over the head, they must be straightened to dig into the vertical air, and the arms brought forward again into their original position. If this is not done quickly enough, a second back loop, or an untidy part of one will result. This is very funny to observe, but not conducive to progression!

If the back loop has been achieved evenly, the student will become stable on their original heading; any uneven input during the manoeuvre will result in a simultaneous turn. Once again the altimeter is checked and a second loop attempted if altitude allows.

DIFFERENT EXITS

Up until now, the student will have been leaving the aircraft in the 'poised' exit position. Depending on the type of aircraft, they will either have been sitting on the door sill, facing the airflow and releasing in a head-up position, or standing outside the aircraft on a step over the wheel, ready to release square to the airflow. Now, as their confidence grows, it is time to try some other exits that involve a different orientation on the slipstream.

An essential exercise, both to boost their confidence further and to demonstrate control, is the unstable exit. In skydiving terms, instability indicates a loss of control in free fall, and this exit will intentionally put them in an unstable situation so that they can effect a recovery. The exercise must be performed from an altitude that will give enough time for the recovery and not put undue pressure on the student, who is probably quite nervous about the whole thing!

Usually kneeling at the door facing the rear of the aircraft at about 45 degrees, the student will pitch forward, somersaulting on to the slipstream. A tumble will result, and some degree of disorientation. After holding a tucked position for five seconds or so, the student reverts to a conventional spread position with as hard an arch as possible. Immediately they will stabilize on the vertical airflow. This is the beauty of the stable position: it will always seek the line of least resistance through the air, in the same way as a shuttlecock or an arrow.

Once stable, the altimeter is checked and, if time allows, other exercises can be attempted. The confidence gained by this exercise is invaluable to later progression. Ask any student which single jump in the progression system was the most enjoyable, and they will probably indicate this skydive.

Now they are ready to start diving from the aircraft. A dive exit is quick and easy, but, like the back loop, is a transitional manoeuvre. The body must be flown

Unstable!

Dive exit as the slipstream takes effect.

through it, changing shape on the slipstream as necessary.

The set up is much the same as for the unstable exit, but the knee at the front of the door should be raised so that the chest and thighs can be presented to the air on release. I ask students to imagine a 45-degree waterfall flowing down past the door to the rear of the aircraft. When they release, they will simply lay themselves on to this waterfall and fly down it. It will naturally level out at the bottom of the slipstream as they convert to the vertical air.

The arms must be extended to grab as

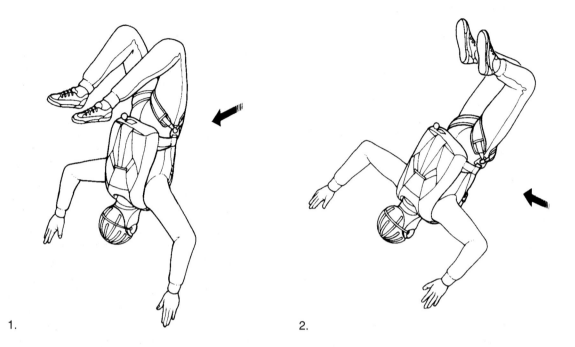

1.

2.

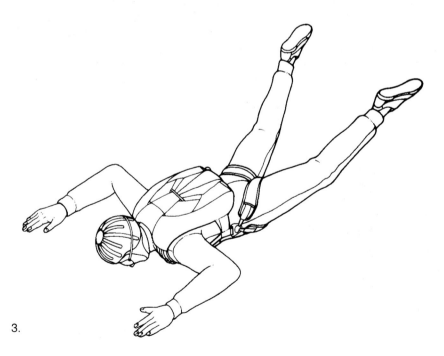

3.

*Progression through
a dive exit. The
arrow denotes
direction of airflow.*

much air as possible on release, and simultaneously, the legs thrown back and bent at the knee. The tendency is to pitch very upright as they go, and if the legs are too straight, a forward tumble can result. The instant that the transition to vertical air begins, the legs are extended and the arms bought back to a normal position. If the student enters the vertical air still in a dive exit position, then they will pitch upright and tumble or turn. As with the back loop, the timing is critical, and sometimes it takes a couple of attempts to get the 'knack'.

TRACKING

A track is a manoeuvre that involves a skydiver making fast horizontal movement across the sky. Once again, this can be done for its own sake, although the most practical application of the exercise is as a means of gaining horizontal separation from fellow jumpers at the end of a formation skydive. This is done in order to gain enough clear sky in which to open your own canopy. About five seconds' tracking is all that is needed usually, but when the exercise is learned, in a student context, it is practised from altitude, and for much longer.

After an exit at 9,000–10,000ft (2,700–3,000m), the student picks a heading in the middle distance, a little way below their horizon. When enough vertical speed has built up, they check their altimeter and move into the track.

Both arms are swept back with the palms down so that they are about 6in (15cm) from the hips. At the same time the legs are straightened and brought closer together with the toes pointed. This will produce a slightly head-down attitude, and if the position was held, forward movement would be achieved simply by the jumper planing forward on the air. However, the secret of an efficient track is to actually produce lift in the same way as an aircraft wing or ram-air canopy. This is done by rolling the shoulders and 'sucking' in the chest as the manoeuvre is initiated. This will round off the back and produce a very crude aerofoil section. Thus, horizontal movement is increased proportional to the distance fallen.

In an efficient position, the resultant increase in speed is huge. Horizontal speeds of 60mph (100km/h) or more are possible. The trick to this exercise is not to bring the limbs too close together, and not to try to

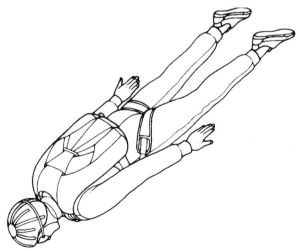

The track.

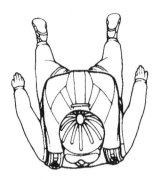

Track from front...

...into a right turn.

de-arch too much. This tends to produce a very steep angle of fall and makes the track inefficient.

Typically, a student will track for about twelve to fifteen seconds on each attempt. In order for the heading to be maintained, all limbs must move evenly and symmetrically, and be held with a degree of tension to cope with the increased airspeed. At the end of the exercise, the student 'flares', simply by re-assuming a normal position. They will generally be struck by the momentary increase of force on the limbs, and a little surprised by the amount of altitude lost during the exercise.

Because we all have different limb pro-

portions, everyone eventually finds their own ideal tracking position. This is one exercise where the actual aesthetics are unimportant compared to the desired effect.

Occasionally, when tracking at the end of a formation skydive, it may be necessary to initiate a turn whilst tracking. If someone has strayed into your flight path, or opened a canopy right in front of you, sudden and decisive action is needed to avoid a collision. Therefore track turns are also taught at this stage. Once speed has been built up in a straight track, the shoulder is ducked in the direction the student wishes to turn. Because of the increased air speed, only a small movement is required. Usually the instructor, who might be flying right along-side, is looking for a sharp 45-degree turn, as this has more effect in a real avoidance situation than a lazy 180-degree change of heading.

Before being cleared from student status, a consolidation dive is performed that links turns, back loops and tracking. This is performed from a high altitude, but always with time and altitude constraints that force the student to discipline themselves enough to complete the dive without fear of opening too low.

AFF PROGRESSION

A typical progression in an AFF format is as follows.

Ground School

To complete a minimum of six hours' ground preparation and a written test.

Level One

1. Exit

Tracking.

2. Circle of awareness (COA) consisting of Ground (pick up a ground heading), Altitude (read altimeter), Secondary (communicate with secondary instructor), Primary (communicate with primary instructor)
3. Three practice pulls
4. COA
5. Free time (ground, altitude, relax)
6. 6,000ft – keep looking at altimeter
7. 5,500ft – pull, safety count, check canopy.

Level Two

1. Exit and COA
2. One practice pull
3. Check altitude – if above 6,000ft, right 90-degree turn
4. Check altitude – if above 6,000ft, move forward for five seconds
5. Free time
6. 6,000ft – shake head to indicate no more work
7. 5,000ft – pull, safety count, check canopy.

Level Three

1. Exit and COA
2. One practice pull
3. COA
4. Free time (instructors release student)
5. 6,000ft – shake head to indicate no more work
6. 5,500ft – pull, safety count, check canopy.

Level Four

only one instructor
1. Exit and COA
2. Right 90-degree turn
3. Check altitude – if above 6,000ft communicate with instructor and react to turn signal

4. Left 90-degree turn
5. Free time
6. 6,000ft – shake head
7. 5,000ft – wave, pull, safety count, check canopy.

Level Five

1. Exit and COA
2. Instructor flies in front of student and gives turn signal
3. 360-degree turn to right
4. Check altitude – if above 6,000ft, communicate with instructor
5. 360-degree turn to left
6. Free time
7. 6,000ft – shake head
8. 5,000ft – wave, pull, safety count, check canopy.

Level Six

1. Solo exit, COA, look for instructor
2. Back loop one
3. Check altitude – if above 6,000ft look for instructor
4. Back loop two
5. Check altitude
6. Track one
7. 6,000ft – shake head

8. 5,000ft – wave, pull, safety count, check canopy.

Level Seven

1. Solo dive exit
2. Student checks own altitude and completes skydive without reference to the instructor
3. Back loop
4. Check altitude
5. Right 360-degree turn
6. Check altitude
7. Left 360-degree turn
8. Check altitude
9. Track and track turn
10. 6,000ft – shake head
11. 5,000ft – wave, pull, safety count and check canopy.

Level Eight

Student to exit aircraft and pull, stable, within ten seconds.

Bear in mind that this format is only an example and that all schools will have their own preferences as to the exact content of any particular skydive.

7 A Choice of Disciplines

To complete any skydiving progression system requires a great degree of commitment from the student. This commitment expresses itself not just in financial terms, but also in the persistence that they must show to overcome learning difficulties, and to sit through a great number of bad weather weekends. Their frustrations are usually swept aside however, by the sense of achievement they feel as they are cleared from student status and onto the dizzy heights of an intermediate skydiver.

They are now presented with a choice of disciplines. Like many weekend jumpers, they may decide to learn and practise two or more of these, and gain a level of competence that allows them maximum enjoyment. Many skydivers, however, feel drawn to one particular discipline and practise it to the exclusion of all else. If the eventual aim is to compete, this is certainly the way to go.

Most of the skills we are about to examine have a structured learning system of their own, and the recent intermediate skydiver, with the basic skills safely 'in the bank', now finds themself at the bottom of another learning tree that they must climb.

FORMATION SKYDIVING

Also known as 'relative work', this discipline is by far the most widely practised form of skydiving. By definition, it requires a skydiver to fall or fly relative to one or more of their fellows during free fall. After a progression over a number of jumps, during which time they will have been introduced to the skills peculiar to this discipline, the intermediate skydiver is introduced to small group flying. This involves an introduction to sequential relative work, where a formation of a certain shape is built in free fall, and then transitioned to another, and another, until the sequence has been completed. The sequence is then repeated as many times as possible until free-fall time runs out.

Most of the formations practised are internationally recognized, as are the transition moves between the formations. This is so that, in competition, teams can be given the same skydives and judged against a common template. The novice formation skydiver will be introduced to a number of different aspects of this discipline during training.

'Dirt diving'

Any skydive must be thoroughly practised on the ground prior to enplaning. In free fall, there is no opportunity to stop and reassess if something goes wrong, so the skydive must be simulated on the ground repeatedly. The process used to achieve this is called dirt diving, and is a skill in itself. All skydives have one organizer, either the team leader, or initially the instructor, and they will conduct the dirt dive.

A 16-way from below.

In order to lay out a formation on the ground, so that it will take on a realistic shape and size, slides or trolleys are used. These resemble the small wheeled platforms that mechanics use to investigate the underside of motorcars! When used on a flat surface, these enable the jumper to lie face down in the same orientation he or she will use in the air. Their fellow skydivers will now appear a realistic distance away, and at a realistic angle.

Formation skydiving jumpsuits have a number of grips on the arms and legs. These provide a reference for the correct place to hold during a formation. Moving around on the trolleys during a dirt dive will enable the jumpers to turn, or move as required, to fly their bodies on to the next correct grip. Thus, a mental sequence is acquired that will be committed to memory and, hopefully, become almost automatic.

Dirt diving illustrates that the mental aspect of skydiving is as important as the physical. If a skydive is not worked out sufficiently on the ground, 'brainlock' can result in the air. This condition is common to all levels of experience. Sometimes, in free fall, in the heat of the moment, the next formation or transition is forgotten by one or more participants. If the memory sequence is not quickly reacquired, then chaos results. Depending at what level one is skydiving, brainlock can result in a wasted jump, or the loss of a competition.

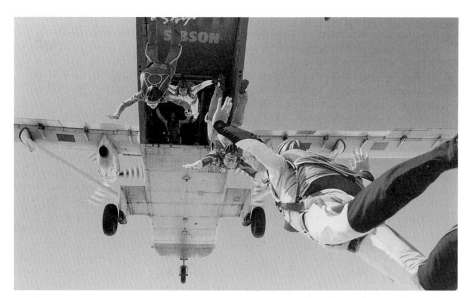

A 4-way free-flown (un-linked) exit...

...flown to a no-contact star.

In order to overcome this handicap, and to provide a format for the organization of sequential skydiving, a system called PAKS is commonly used. This is an acronym for:

Picture. **A**ngles. **K**eys. **S**ecret stuff!

Initially the **picture** is acquired. The skydive is walked or trolleyed through repeat-

edly, until all participants have a clear mental sequence committed to memory.

Then the **angles** are worked out. The particular angle at which a jumper must fly relative to their fellows is important. Can your arms physically reach the grips you need? Will the angle you are at in one formation enable you to smoothly transition to the next without unnessecary time loss?

One-to-one formation skydiving coaching.

'Dirt-diving' a 9-way opposed diamond.

4-way in transition.

Keys are the signals given by one member, when a formation has been completed, to transition to the next. The person giving the keys may change throughout the skydive, depending on who is in the best position to see everything. On larger group skydives, this role can be sub-delegated to various individuals who will look at the relevant person when their section has been completed. A key is given by a sharp, significant nod of the head, or in some cases where eye contact is impossible, a shake.

Secret stuff is harder to explain. Experienced teams will sometimes use their own methods of transition, or efficient ways of doing things that they will not want to share in competition. Most of the secret stuff of past years has now filtered down into general skydiving coaching, and has been used to the benefit of all. Skydiving is unique in the way that experienced teams are generally free with information and will share it with anyone who asks. Some of the current cutting-edge techniques and methods, however, are being used in competition as we speak, and I cannot detail them here because ... well, they're secret!

Fall Rate Control

This is just about the most important skill to be acquired by the novice formation skydiver. For two or more people to fall on a level, relative to one another, they must have a constant fall rate. Heavier people fall faster, lighter people fall slower, and while a team may eventually address this problem by resorting to weight vests, any jumper must know how to alter their fall rate while remaining in the neutral stable position.

Anyone in a relaxed, arched skydiving position will fall at a given speed. Their fall rate can be adjusted simply by changing the resistance they present to the vertical airflow. To increase fall rate, it is simply necessary to arch more. Drawing the shoulders and thighs back from the relative air, and pushing the hips downwards, increases the shuttlecock effect of the body, and the vertical descent rate increases. Consequently, removing some of the body's natural arch will slow the jumper down. Some slow-fall situations call for a simple flattening of the body to match a slow-falling formation, while some situations call for a more radical de-arch. If the skydiver has allowed themself to sink well below the level of everybody else, they need to do something about it quickly. Keeping their limbs still spread to the basic position, they will cup air, rolling the shoulders forward and dropping the knees. The effect is like trying to hug a large beach ball. To de-arch as radically as possible is to be teetering on the edge of instability, and everybody has their own way of doing it most efficiently. The best solution however, is not to have gone below the formation in the first place!

As the intermediate skydiver learns these skills with their instructor on a one-to-one basis, they must learn to control their fall rate without inducing any lateral movement. They must learn to fly 'in the tube', balancing on their own vertical column of air.

Forward Movement

We have looked at radical forward movement in the form of tracking. Now it must be

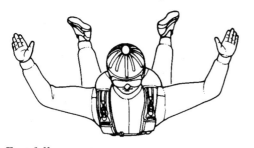

Fast fall.

Increased arch makes the air softer.

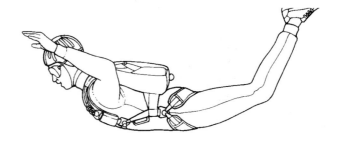

learned in a much more subtle way. In any form of formation skydiving, a jumper will often need to punch their body forward slightly in order to fly on to someone's grips. This is done simply by extending the legs slightly over the top of the knees, thus increasing resistance to the lower body and planing the jumper forwards. The greater the extension, the greater the effect. Because a degree of height loss accompanies all forward movement, the skydiver must be prepared to adjust their fall rate with the shape of the body during any approach. This is one example of combining skills to achieve an objective. The forward movement, providing it is not too great, can be stopped simply by neutralizing the position again, although the arms can be used to brake if momentum has built up.

In-Place Turns

At this level, the skydiver has already learned to turn accurately, changing their heading at will to face where they wish. Now they find they must modify their technique somewhat in order to change formation as quickly as possible. If they have learned to turn by themselves in free fall, they may not be aware that they are actually covering ground laterally while the manoeuvre is happening. This 'sliding' happens because they are not turning around a central point, i.e. their hips and centre of gravity. Turns using the upper body alone result in this. Now, leg input must be applied simultaneously by tilting both lower legs over in the direction of turn. This will result in a true propeller turn, and the body will remain in place, and grips may be taken immediately, instead of applying lateral movement to make up the ground lost.

Linked Exits – 'Launching'

Up until now, the skydiver has left the aircraft by themselves to perform solo exercises. Now, as they learn the rudiments of formation skydiving, they will be introduced to the exacting skill of launching the formation from the aircraft door while linked together. Some skydives, particularly the larger formations, will necessarily require individuals to leave separately, flying down to the base formation before docking. Most

small-group skydiving, particularly the disciplines of four- and eight-person sequential, will require the team to launch as one group. This is done to save working time. If the first specified formation cannot actually be launched, it can quickly be transitioned to, simply by changing grips as the group leave the aircraft. There are assigned positions during a launch.

The 'rear floaters' will climb outside the aircraft at the back of the door using a purpose-built rail. Hanging on with one hand, they will rotate to face the slipstream or relative air, and take up a grip on an arm or a leg. The 'front floaters' will do the same at the front of the door, the 'centre floaters' will then position themselves in between. Meanwhile, the 'divers' have been crouching inside the aircraft facing out, taking appropriate grips on the floaters. Thus, the formation is ready to launch. Sometimes, because of the increased tension created, harness grips are taken instead of jumpsuit

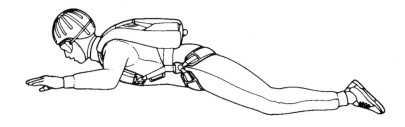

Slow fall.

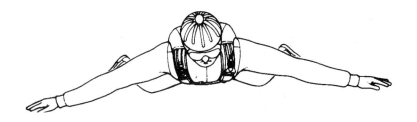

Negative arch makes the air harder.

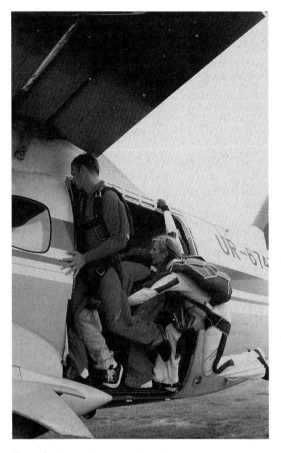

Dirt-diving a 4-way exit.

grips. This also frees the arms to fly on the air.

An exit count is given by the appropriate member. This is generally a 'ready, set, go' accompanied by a physical pulse or 'rock'. Communication is vital for a simultaneous launch, and due to the noise level of the aircraft and wind, eye contact is of prime importance. As the formation drops on to the air, the skydive is under way, and as quickly as possible, the first formation achieved.

At the end of every formation skydive, well before the pull altitude of around 2,500ft (750m), the group must turn away

from each other and perform their track. This is the true application of the skill discussed previously, and provides each skydiver with enough clear air in which to open their canopy. The larger the formation, the higher the 'break-off' altitude. Although 3,500ft (1,000m) is the norm, larger formations tend to break off in waves from about 5,500ft (1,700m) downwards.

These are the basic skills involved in sequential formation skydiving. Such has been the increase in skill level around the world over recent years, that sixteen-person teams are now achieving the same amount of formations or 'points' on a given skydive, as their four-person counterparts were a few short years ago.

Some skydivers prefer larger formations still, and will travel the world in search of larger formation loads. When a formation exceeds a certain size, several aircraft are required to achieve it, and the organization level needed is commensurately greater. At the time of writing, the first British 100-person formation had just been achieved, and the world record stands at 297. This discipline has clearly come a long way from the pioneering days of the mid-1960s, when success was measured by the ability to pass a baton between two people as proof of contact!

CANOPY RELATIVE WORK (CRW)

This discipline, younger than its free-fall counterpart, simply takes the principle of relative flight and applies it to the canopy ride instead of the free fall. This aspect of our sport only became possible with the widespread adoption of the ram-air canopy, as the flight characteristics of the old round parachutes simply did not lend themselves to close contact formation flying.

A large formation leaves the tailgate. Chaos!

A 'room dive' – one formation inside another.

Canopies fill the sky after a large formation load.

A CRW diamond formation nearing completion.

Initially, devotees of CRW would tend to practise it during a normal canopy descent after a free-fall formation jump. As the discipline progressed, however, participants would devote the entire jump to it, leaving the aircraft at high altitude, but opening their canopies immediately to maximize the working time. A major advantage of CRW is that everything happens more slowly than in formation skydiving. Working time on each jump is measured in minutes instead of seconds. Also, verbal communication is possible throughout the descent, making teaching and teamwork a lot easier.

The most basic of all CRW formations is the biplane. Having established a heading, the stack pilot, who will eventually steer the formation, will wait for another jumper to fly their canopy's centre cell into the back of their legs. Both will adjust their canopies' speed and lift to achieve this. As the docking occurs, the stack pilot will hook their feet around the centre lines of the other canopy and slide down them until they are in the risers just above the other jumper. The two canopies can now be flown as one, both jumpers choosing to land their formation,

A 2-stack with the third member about to dock.

releasing at the last moment and flaring almost simultaneously. It is common however, to transition to another formation, such as a bi-hand, where both canopies are flown side by side and steered with the outside toggle of each.

Sometimes a down-plane will be built from this. Interlocking legs and steering the canopies away from each other, will encourage them to separate and dive at the ground until the jumpers choose to release. The increase in vertical speed makes this enormous fun to do and thrilling to watch. It generally forms an integral part of any CRW display.

Like its free-fall counterpart, CRW is practised keenly at competition level. Sequential formations are built and judged on the same principles. Rotations are also

performed: a team, usually a unit of four, will build a stack and rotate pilots from top to bottom. This is performed dramatically by the top canopy being stalled so that it partially collapses and falls down the back of the stack. It will be allowed to gain air and fly at the right moment so that it can quickly be re-docked on the bottom. As soon as this is achieved, the process starts again. It is not surprising that some experienced jumpers view CRW with suspicion! Everyone is taught on a basic parachute course to avoid other canopies at all times. Some seem happy to apply that rule throughout their jumping careers. Some don't – they do CRW.

CRW is practised around the world with a high degree of skill and safety. It has its own pitfalls, however, and techniques and equipment have developed to deal with these. The possibility of entanglement is always present, so smooth clothing is worn and accessible knives are worn by all. All transition work will cease by an altitude that gives a margin for emergency drills should they be needed.

STYLE AND ACCURACY – THE 'CLASSICS'

These twin disciplines arose in the very early days of the sport before formation parachuting of any sort was taken seriously. Although their adherents are fewer in number these days, the skills are still practised recreationally and competed in at the highest level.

Individual style consists of a series of free-fall manoeuvres performed as quickly and precisely as possible. The sequence of manoeuvres is known as a 'series'. A 'right' series would consist of:

1. Right 360-degree turn, left 360-degree turn, back loop;
2. Right 360-degree turn, left 360-degree turn, back loop.

Alternatives are a 'left' series, starting with turns to the left, or a 'cross' series, alternating directions.

As we have seen, any free-fall manoeuvre is performed more easily if the jumper is falling quickly; therefore a position was developed that is peculiar to this branch of the sport: the 'style tuck'. As the style jumper exits the aircraft on heading, they will initially dive for several seconds to build up a high vertical speed, and suddenly they will tuck. The knees are drawn up to the chest and both arms bent and pulled in close to the body. Although this position sounds similar to a de-arch or slow-fall posi-

tion, it is not, being far more radical, and actually increasing descent rate rather than reducing it.

The air at this time feels very hard because of the increased speed, and only small movements are now required to induce a rapid turn. In practice and competition, undershoots and overshoots are common because of the difficulty in stopping the turn at the correct moment. These are penalized. Likewise, banking during the turn is not considered good style, it being preferable to remain horizontally aligned throughout. A back loop will immediately follow, once again being stopped before any pitching up occurs. The jumper will now perform the second half of their series.

To give some idea of the proficiency that can be achieved, consider that a student free-faller will be taught to turn 360 degrees in about four to five seconds, whereas in style competition, an entire series is routinely done in under seven!

Canopy accuracy is a sister discipline to style, and jumpers who practise one are generally quite proficient in the other. Accuracy is, of course, practised to some extent by every skydiver on every jump, including their first. As we have seen, it is a basic parachuting skill to be able to land a canopy in an intended safe area. Accuracy takes this skill to extremes, the target being a 3cm (1in)-diameter disc in the middle of an electronic pad. As contact is made by the jumper's heel or toe, a readout gives the distance from the centre of the disc and the parachutist is judged accordingly.

Accuracy can be practised on just about any canopy, but the smaller, more radical parachutes that are favoured by many skydivers today are less than ideal. Canopies designed specifically for this discipline tend to be large, and trimmed to perform predictably in deep brakes, for it is in this configuration that the jumper will attack the target. Haphazard spirals and radical turns close to the ground form no part of the accuracy jumper's repertoire; instead, they will set up some distance downwind of the pad at sufficient height to give room for adjustments, and commence a forward descent down an imaginary wire towards the target. During this final approach, they will adjust the angle of approach using the toggles as brakes. Care is needed as the canopy is now operating in an area close to the stall known as the 'sink'. Finally, a point is reached directly over the target, and the chosen foot is placed on to the disc. Foot placement is an art in itself, and the competitor will often need to make a split-second decision to use either their heel or toe, depending on whether an overshoot or undershoot has occurred.

As a consequence of their chosen discipline, accuracy jumpers tend to understand their parachute's performance intimately, and develop an ability to detect small changes in wind speed and direction more readily than the average recreational skydiver.

Accuracy landings are not pretty, and rarely result in a stand-up. It is necessary, therefore, that the pad is surrounded by a soft area. Traditionally this has been a pea-gravel pit some 30m (100ft) in diameter. More recently, with the advent of mobile competition venues, a padded 'tuft' is used instead.

FREESTYLE, FREEFLYING AND SKYSURFING – THE 'NEW AGE' DISCIPLINES

If style and accuracy can be considered to be the elder statesmen of our sport, then the new age disciplines named above are the new kids on the block. Brash, colourful and still undergoing much experimentation, they arose out of a reaction to the precise

A freeflyer with video.

conventional disciplines that were perceived by some as restrictive and altogether too regimented. This doesn't mean that these newer skills are any less demanding, far from it. In order to be truly proficient, participants need a high degree of fitness and flexibility, and to be keenly aware of the various associated safety skills.

Freestyle can be likened to conventional style in that there are set moves and positions to be adopted and performed throughout the skydive. It does, however, provide for freedom of expression and imagination, and in this respect can be likened to ice skating or similar sports. Every free-fall discipline now uses air-to-air video as a means of coaching and judging. In freestyle, the difference is that the video cameraperson is a performing member of the team, performing rolls and loops and changing their vertical orientation around their teammate in order to enhance the appearance of the skydive. The results are never

less than impressive. The over-used term 'aerial ballet' was never more true, with some top international competitors cross-training in various dance disciplines as well as skydiving.

Freeflying is just that, the freedom to leave an aircraft and do whatever you wish during the free-fall time available. The skill of falling vertically head-down has now been mastered, along with stand-up and sitting techniques and the transitions in between.

Because most freestyle and freeflying positions involve presenting less surface area to the air than conventional flat flying, greater average speeds are achieved and the free-fall time per jump is considerably less. It is for this reason that altitude awareness is critical to these disciplines. Audible altimeters are considered essential, as are AADs. Free-fall collisions in any aspect of our sport are rare because of the attention to detail paid when we teach

Sit flying at the start of a freestyle dive.

Freeflying.

disciplined flying. A collision during a freefly jump, however, can have particularly serious consequences, and teaching must be tailored to the individual student's ability, with care taken before they are allowed to jump unsupervised with others.

Skysurfing is probably familiar to anyone with a TV set. It is the most recent, media-friendly incarnation of our sport, appearing both exciting and skilful. Until fairly recently, skysurfing was practised by relatively few jumpers. Now, as techniques are perfected and passed on, teaching structures are becoming formalized, and equipment perfected.

The skysurfer will launch themself upright from the aircraft, presenting the bottom of their board to the relative air. They will fly down the slipstream as though it were a wave, though unlike its aquatic counterpart, upright is not the only option. Because the board is actually attached to the skysurfer's feet, they are able to loop,

Skysurfing exit.

Spinning the board.

roll and turn as well as gaining fast horizontal movement when desired. Competition is judged in much the same way as for freestyle, using a free-fall video person to fly with – and complement – the surfer's moves.

Surfers will begin their learning process on small boards and progress to larger ones as their technique improves. Though the board is attached with bindings to the jumper's feet, they can choose to release it at any time via a cutaway cable. This may be necessary in the event of an irrecoverable loss of control in free fall, or a canopy malfunction.

All aspects of the sport within this chapter can be practised competitively or just for fun. We will now examine some non-competitive directions that the newly experienced skydiver may choose become involved in.

8   Other Advanced Skills

The skills detailed here can be practised recreationally or professionally. They are in no way a natural progression for any skydiver, simply aspects of the sport that they can choose to participate in if they wish.

QUALIFIED INSTRUCTOR

One thing is for certain, if there were no instructors, there would be no skydivers. No skydiver jumping today worked things out from scratch by themself. If it were not for a steady influx of experienced jumpers gaining instructor's ratings year by year, bringing with them new ideas and a new slant on old ones, the sport would very quickly become stale and die.

Every national body has a means of ratifying experienced jumpers as instructors and, even before this process begins, the prospective candidate will, under supervision, probably start working with students at their own centre and getting involved in various aspects of coaching. Here they will begin to get an idea of the patience necessary as they very quickly discover that almost no one is a natural skydiver. Sometimes even the fittest, most intelligent of people have difficulty mastering some practical or theoretical aspect of a skill.

The instructor's role is threefold. Firstly, they must have the knowledge to teach a skill, putting the information across in a way that it will be understood. This will not be the same for every student. Secondly, they must be able to watch that skill being practised, both on the ground and in the air, identify any mistakes made, and give corrective input so that the error will not be repeated. Finally, they are responsible for the legislative aspect of the sport: making sure that any survival skills are practised as often as necessary, and that a student is not progressed faster than they are legally allowed to be. Any instructor or coach must be progressive and encouraging, building confidence in their pupils, and never forgetting that at some times, the people they are responsible for will be very scared. This is most marked in the case of a first-jump student, who will react correctly or incorrectly to situations depending on how much confidence they have in themselves, and how deep their training has been. This confidence is directly related to the faith they put in their instructors and equipment.

A good instructor will teach from the heart as well as the head, sympathizing, encouraging and imposing their personality on to every aspect of their work. It is hard work, always challenging, but the rewards are enormous. It never fails to give me a buzz to look at, and listen to, a first-jump student returning to the packing shed. Likewise at some later date, to see that person qualify as an experienced jumper – knowing that they are partly a product of your teaching.

Most skydiving authorities issue advanced instructor ratings. These qualify the holder to administer more advanced aspects of the sport such as night jumps and water jumps. They also allow the holder to become a Chief Instructor, responsible for every aspect of drop zone management and skydiving operations.

A further stage is that of Examiner. Residential courses are held at some centres for the purpose of ratifying new instructors, and these are administered by qualified examiners. It is not always the case that an excellent skydiver makes an excellent instructor. It is no good having the knowledge if one lacks the expression to put it across, or the patience and understanding to work with a student who is not absorbing the information quickly enough.

Most national skydiving organizations have a safety committee of some sort whose job it is to monitor the teaching infrastructure of that country. They will receive input on new techniques and equipment, and investigate how they can be applied 'in the field' by individual centres. They will also research any incidents or problems that have been bought to their attention, and advise or legislate accordingly.

RIGGING

All experienced skydivers need a thorough working knowledge of their equipment. As they progress through their student days and subsequent chosen disciplines, they will absorb this knowledge through periods of formal packing instruction and time spent learning how to 'flight line check' other parachutists prior to enplaning. Some jumpers, however, develop a profound interest in the technical side of parachute equipment. If we use the analogy of the motor car, most of us are content to drive and conduct routine maintenance without ever becoming mechanics. We are content to leave the more difficult tasks to somebody qualified. The same is true in the world of skydiving. A rigger is licensed to inspect and repair most items of equipment. A further qualification of master rigger enables the holder to perform structural work on reserve canopies and harness/container systems. Most large parachute centres have a rigger on site, providing a maintenance facility and avoiding the need for jumpers to refer back to the manufacturer whenever something needs attention.

Every jumper needs to be able to pack their main canopy, but most are content to turn their equipment over to a rigger when a reserve re-pack is required. Some governing bodies keep this exacting skill in the domain of the rigger, and some issue advanced packing qualifications to experienced jumpers who will attend a detailed course prior to gaining them.

Reserve parachutes are rarely used, but all require periodic re-packs and inspections. Depending on where they are used, these inspections are done on a four- or six-monthly cycle. They are necessary for two reasons:

- To detect any contamination inside the container that is invisible from the outside. On rare occasions, airborne or liquid contaminants have been found that attack the material of the canopy, lines, or metalwork. A regular re-pack will also ensure that the canopy does not become too 'bedded' in the container.

- If ever an error has occurred during the reserve packing process, it will never go more than one re-pack cycle without being discovered.

Once packed, an entry will be made in the

reserve log that accompanies every para-chute system. This is kept with the rig at all times: it gives the date of the next re-pack, and details of any maintenance carried out at the time.

PACKING

Although skydivers routinely pack their own main canopies, there are occasions when they may want to engage the services of a professional. Skydivers take skydiving holidays! And whereas they might happily pack their gear on their home drop zone, if one is involved in the intensive jumping of a 'boogie' – as skydiving festivals are often known – particularly in a hot climate, it is pleasant to take a holiday from the routine of packing as well. This facility is ideally suited to competition teams, who will usu-ally attend an intensive training camp prior to an important competition, making up to ten jumps per day. Between jumps, their time is better occupied debriefing the previ-ous skydive and preparing for the next one.

There are two common methods of pack-ing a canopy: 'flat' packing and 'pro' packing. Flat packing is the traditional method, usu-ally used with large student canopies, where the initial stages can be checked and inspected more easily, and where individual checks have to be signed for and recorded. This method involves laying the canopy on a suitable clean surface, initially on its side, and condensing the cells so that a tight bun-dle can be made before the canopy is squeezed into its deployment bag. Pro pack-ing is used for the newer, smaller canopies usually constructed of zero-porosity fabric. In this method, the parachute is hung over the packer's shoulder and the cells folded, or 'flaked' while the canopy is off the ground. Zero-porosity fabric is more difficult to con-trol during the packing process and this

method makes the procedure easier and neater.

With either method, the canopy is checked at four stages. In the case of a stu-dent parachute, where accountability is needed, these checks will be entered by sig-nature in a logbook. When packing for one-self, or for an experienced jumper, the checks will be done along the way without stopping. The checks are:

Check one The canopy is laid out and all necessary components checked. The lines are inspected for tangles that may have

'Pro' packing.

occurred after landing and the material is inspected for rips, scuffs or friction burns. Steering toggle knots and connector links are checked as secure.

Check two The canopy has been folded ready to be put into the bag. All material has been cleared from the lines and the slider is pulled up and correctly positioned. The brakes have been set.

Check three The canopy has been put in the bag and the suspension lines are stowed. All elastic bands or 'bungees' are in good condition and strong enough to do their job. The deployment bag is usually positioned in the main container at this stage.

Check four The container is closed and all its components are in good condition. The rig is in every respect ready to jump.

The fact that parachutes open correctly almost all of the time is no accident. The safety record we enjoy today is the result of manufacturers' research and development programmes, the integrity of those licensed to repair and maintain equipment, and the fact that those involved in packing generally never forget that the quality of their work is the difference between a perfect canopy and a malfunction.

DISPLAY PARACHUTING

Very often, the first exposure that a member of the public has to our sport is as a spectator at a parachuting display. Displays can vary enormously in scale. A demonstration may consist of three or four members of a local club jumping into the village fête as a public relations exercise, or it can be a large affair, performed for a corporate function,

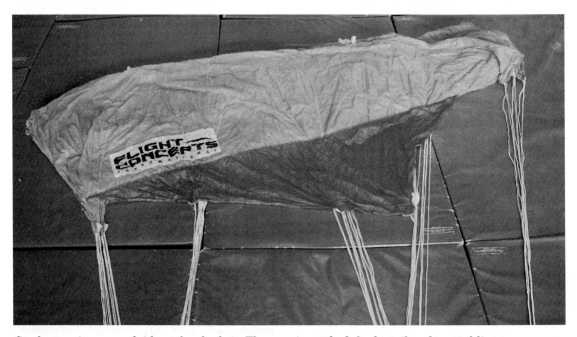

Student main canopy laid out for check 1. The nose is on the left, the tail and control lines are on the right.

Packing check 2.

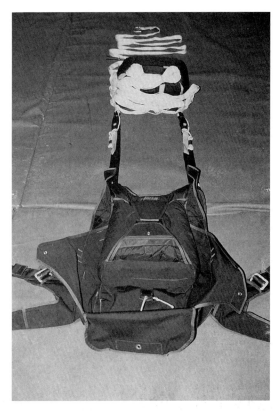

Packing check 3.

employing a professional team who will demonstrate several different aspects of the sport.

As visually thrilling as free fall is to its participants, a spectator on the ground will find it hard to see the detail of a skydiving formation. They may have difficulty seeing the jumpers at all, due to the altitude at which these manoeuvres are performed. Therefore, it is the canopy ride that can be best displayed. Canopy formation flying and accuracy are generally the most appropriate aspects of parachuting within this discipline. An experienced jumper may think nothing of landing their canopy easily within an arena measuring just 300ft (100m) on each side. However, to the uninitiated – some of whom harbour the impres-

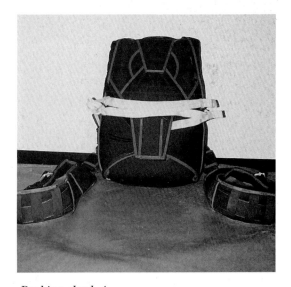

Packing check 4.

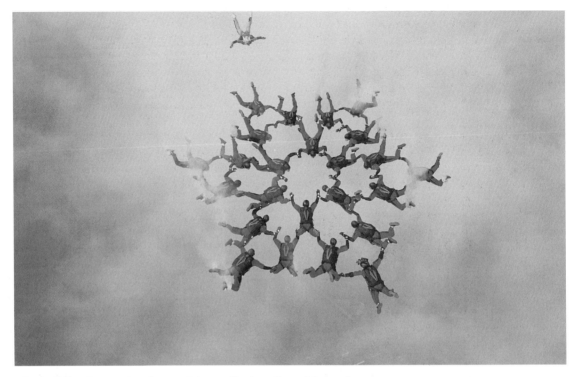

The Red Devils team perform a 24-way display dive with smoke.

sion that we float haphazardly to earth each time and exert almost no control over where we land – this is an almost superhuman feat!

This is not to infer that display parachuting is easy. It is one thing to land accurately on each jump when one has the luxury of a large, dedicated drop zone with several acres of overshoot. It is psychologically different, however, when your drop zone for the day is surrounded by buildings, busy roads, and has several hundred spectators, keen to encroach upon your safe area for a closer look!

It is for this reason that displays are organized on a very disciplined basis, and those who take part in them are trained and qualified to do so. All display teams will have a nominated leader who is responsible for every aspect of the organization. The team will also be registered with the sport's governing body and the appropriate civil aviation authority.

Once an approach has been made by the organizer, a visit will be made to the venue. This is simply to ascertain if the landing area is physically large enough to safely jump into. Most arenas look vastly different on the initial 'recce' to how they will appear on the day. A large field can shrink significantly when stalls, beer tents, 700 spectators and a car park have been added. Therefore, the organizer must be questioned in detail as to how the venue will appear on the day, and told the minimum dimensions of the clear area that the team will require.

Another purpose of the recce is to provide an altimeter setting. If the display is to be made on to higher or lower ground than that of the home airfield, this must be taken into account. For example, if the arena was 400ft lower than the take-off field, the team would set their altimeters at plus 400ft. This would give them an accurate height reading above the venue when they arrived overhead.

The next stage of preparation is the briefing. This will include not just the team of jumpers, but the ground party and pilot as well. Every display needs to have a drop zone controller in the same way as any normal parachuting site, and they must be briefed as to any specific duties along with the team. The briefing will include a representation of the drop zone, either as a photograph or sketch. The team will have planned what type of jump they intend to do, but need to be briefed on any particular hazards peculiar to that venue. Large buildings or structures upwind of the arena can pose a problem because of the related turbulence that can extend quite a distance downwind. In the same way, a large crowd can create heat turbulence of its own. The weather will be constantly monitored. If the display is some distance from the take-off field, the conditions can be significantly different, another reason why liaison with the ground party is important.

After the briefing, the drop zone controller and their team will leave for the venue. They must get there well before the team arrive overhead. If previous events in the arena are overrunning, or the drop zone turns out to be a third of its intended size, the display may have to be delayed or even, in the worst event, be cancelled. All being well, however, they will set up a windsock or similar means of wind indication for the team. Usually, a large orange cross is placed in the centre of the arena as a focal point for accuracy, and a smoke canister made ready to be fired as the team open their canopies.

The drop zone controller will now make radio contact with the aircraft.

All good display teams have a commentator whose job it is to lead the spectators through the display as things happen. The commentator is a very important part of the team: a good one can make even a mundane display seem like the most exciting thing ever witnessed, and a bad one can easily take the shine off a professionally staged exhibition.

A wind drift indicator will be dropped as for normal parachuting, and an opening point determined. Sometimes, if the cloudbase is at a lower than ideal altitude, the plan may have to be changed and any freefall exercises discarded in favour of a short delay and canopy ride. A disciplined team will never jump regardless of weather conditions just to avoid disappointing their audience. In this branch of our sport, like any other, safety for skydivers and public alike must be the most important factor.

All being well, the aircraft will now run in and the team will jump. The excitement that the spectators feel as they watch the skydivers in free fall, seemingly delaying for ever before opening their canopies, is matched by the jumpers themselves, who can see the arena as a small green area the size of a postage stamp surrounded by major roads, housing estates and factories! Smoke canisters attached to ankle brackets are a good way to keep the free-fallers visible, and provide a sense of speed prior to opening, increasing the apparent drama of what is happening. All being well, which it usually is, the demonstration will conclude with each member making a pinpoint, stand-up landing on the target cross to applause from all concerned.

Most experienced jumpers are keen to do displays. The general public don't attend parachuting airfields in great numbers, but a display brings our sport to them, and brings out the extrovert in most parachutists, who are as keen to sign autographs in the beer tent afterwards as they are to actually jump!

Displays, and the attendant recruitment drive that the ground party will instigate, have been responsible for introducing many people to skydiving over the years. Significantly, they help to bridge the public perception of our sport with the reality and, performed correctly, can project skydiving as an adventurous, colourful and safe activity.

CAMERA JUMPING

There can be few sports that can provide a spectacle for the camera in the way that parachuting does. Not only do skydiving formations and canopies give a vividly coloured and textured subject matter, but they are photographed and filmed against the most vivid backdrops conceivable.

Parachuting photography is as old as the sport itself, with most of the grainy images of the early pioneers being taken from the ground or the aircraft as the jumper fell away. It wasn't long, however, before someone came up with the idea of fixing a camera to their helmet, and attempting to capture the action as it happened. Throughout the 1960s, free-fall photography progressed. While some jumpers preferred to take stills, many favoured the medium of film, making mounts for their helmets to take either 8mm or 16mm cameras. Several dedicated free-fall documentary shorts made during the late 1960s and early 1970s became classics within the skydiving world. For the first time, we could capture the drama and excitement of the sport and show it to everyone! Despite being clearly very dated now, these films are still very popular among jumpers. Although the skills portrayed are

Camera helmet with stills and video cameras.

very basic compared to today's achievements, they show a golden age of discovery that will never be seen again.

It is important to realize that to be a successful free-fall photographer, whether using stills or the moving image, the skydiver needs to have achieved not only a high level of ability within the sport, but also a similar level of excellence with the camera. There are variables to be considered on each jump. The quality of the light, the position of the sun relative to the subject matter, the fall-rate of the individual or formation, and the need for increased awareness of time elapsed so that both subject and photographer can break off and deploy their canopies at the correct altitude.

As the years have progressed, equipment has been developed and techniques refined

4-way with team cameraman. Note the suit-wings for fall-rate control.

that have made the camera jumper's job a lot easier without detracting from any of the skill involved. Video has replaced film as the preferred medium, and more recently, with the advent of digital cameras, the weight carried on the helmet has reduced dramatically. The reduction of weight carried on the head has always been a priority factor. If, as sometimes happens, a hard opening is experienced, the tendency of the head to 'whiplash', causing severe neck injury, is a risk. Camera jumpers did, and still do to some extent, prefer a canopy that opens softly, and will alter their packing to achieve this. These days, it is likely that a modern helmet, fitted with a light digital video unit, will weigh little more than an older helmet by itself! Modern technology has also proved a boon to stills jumpers, who will take pictures via an electronic shutter release positioned either in their hand or between the teeth.

Audible altimeters have proved ideally suited to this discipline. A video jumper cannot move to check their visual altimeter without losing the subject matter. Therefore, they have previously needed to rely on the other jumpers to break off and track at the correct altitude. Some, over the years, have been taken low by a team that has got carried away with their skydive. An audible altimeter set for break-off altitude now removes this dependency to a great extent. A camera jumper will not normally turn and track at the end of a relative skydive, opening instead in the clear air above the centre of the formation as it breaks up.

During the 1980s, the increase in ability among camera jumpers moved the art into another dual role, that of judge and jury.

Videoing from a sit position.

Formation skydiving competitions had previously been judged from the ground, initially using telemeters, and then ground-to-air video. This format was fine when it was all that was available, but proved sometimes to be less than totally reliable. Rejumps were often awarded to teams who could not be seen sufficiently, or who failed to demonstrate certain formations to the judges' satisfaction. Disputes were common. Air-to-air video was introduced as a secondary judging medium and soon, after having proved its worth, was adopted as the primary judging medium for all national and international competitions.

This meant that the cameraman became part of the team itself. Overnight, four-person formation teams became five, and eight-person teams nine. It was not just in competition itself that the camera became important, but during training also. Because sequential formation skydiving is such a fast discipline, mistakes made dur-

ing the dive, such as wrong grips or incorrect transitions, sometimes cannot be identified at the time. On a video debrief that can be watched repeatedly, however, problems can be identified and corrected by the team or their coach. The ability of the video camera to point its unforgiving finger at individual mistakes has earned it the not so affectionate nickname of 'one-eyed axeman'.

The team video person will generally take up a rear floating slot on the outside of the fuselage, facing forward. As the team form in the door and take up their respective grips, they will begin the exit count accompanied by a mutual 'rock' or pulse. This gives the cameraperson a cue to release at the correct moment. They will usually time their release a split second before the team themselves leave the aircraft, and will surf on the slipstream looking back up at the first point and transition. Once the team has transitioned into vertical air, the camera will be flown as near as possible directly above the formation. This will facilitate a perfect judging angle. A truly vertical perspective is not possible, due to the team's wake turbulence or 'burble' – the area of unstable air in their wake that would cause the camera jumper to fall on top of the team. Therefore, using specially designed jumpsuit wings as well as their honed flying skills to match fall rate and movement, they will hover on the edge of the burble and film until working time has run out.

In a competition, the video will be turned over to the judging panel as soon as possible after landing.

9   Out on the Edge

As we have seen, parachuting and skydiving take many forms and mean different things to different people. In addition to the accepted 'mainstream' elements, there are several disciplines that do not conform to what is considered conventional. These activities assume a higher level of risk to the disciplines we have previously discussed and as such are pursued only by a minority, and for different reasons to the ones normally given for participation in skydiving.

BASE JUMPING

BASE is simply an acronym for 'Buildings, Antennae, Spans and Earth'. In short, skydiving without aircraft! It is viewed with hostility by most national parachuting bodies for the several reasons. Firstly, in situations where a base jumper leaps from a building or similar structure in a highly populated area, it can be argued that the general public are put at risk. Traffic has been thrown into chaos by jumpers landing in busy thoroughfares, and in a situation where the canopy fails to open, it is possible that anyone innocently wandering into the parachutist's descent path would become involved in the tragedy also. This is an entirely justifiable point of view, though the same criticism could be levelled at the more mainstream elements of the sport. Skydivers do not generally seek permission of the people directly below them at the moment of exit!

Another reason that base jumping is frowned upon is that it very often involves trespass. It is unlikely that the owners of a tall office building or radio transmitter mast would allow skydivers to use it for their sport, therefore permission is not sought. The base community is a clandestine one, mostly consisting of regular skydivers who pursue both activities side by side, but also by a few who have never jumped conventionally.

The main problem that people have with base jumping is that most of it happens from a much lower altitude then anyone would sensibly step out of an aircraft. This increases the risk enormously simply because there is no time to deploy a reserve in the event of a canopy malfunction. Also, where buildings are involved, or antenna masts with support cables, there is the risk that an off-heading opening could fly the jumper into the fixed object itself. These factors bring us to the core reason for base jumping. It is the thrill and power of the moment itself, the potential consequences and the sense of achievement afterwards that draws jumpers to this activity. Their motivations are not far removed from those of most skydivers, simply magnified.

None of the above is meant to infer that base jumpers have an inherent death wish. Indeed, most take safety precautions that are in line with the precarious nature of

Jumping the dam.

An instant later, with pilot chute inflation.

their activity. Equipment is manufactured specifically for the discipline with characteristics that target the jumpers requirements:

- A larger than normal pilot chute is used for low-altitude free-fall jumps. This grabs more air and will make for a faster deployment at a time when the jumper does not have the advantage of an aircraft slipstream or an extended delay to provide airspeed. Most jumps made from very low altitudes of 500ft (150m) or less are made with a static line.

111

- Canopies used tend to be seven- instead of nine-cell. This reduces the risk of an off-heading or unpredictable opening.

- The slider, always present on a normal ram-air canopy to slow and moderate the opening shock, is removed for very short delays. This, along with the large pilot chute, means that the canopy will develop very quickly once deployment has begun.

In order to become a true initiate, the base jumper must complete a descent from each one of the four categories of fixed object. Some of these objects themselves have become legendary within the sport. From a green valley in the semi-wilderness of the Yosemite National Park in California rises one of the most striking rock faces on the planet: El Capitan. For a long time the exclusive reserve of rock climbers, this mountain became a Mecca for base jumpers in the late 1970s, and for a period of time, through negotiation with the park services, became legal.

Standing in excess of 3,000ft (900m) above the valley floor, the launch point offers a free-fall delay in excess of ten seconds, and a canopy ride into a relatively large, safe landing field. During the free fall, the jumper would use a track position in order to gain valuable distance from the rock face, a luxury not possible on shorter delays. Unfortunately, for various reasons the permission to jump 'El Cap' has been withdrawn, and it is now a criminal offence to make such an attempt, the penalties being a huge fine and surrender of one's parachuting equipment.

The respectable face of base jumping is seen at the New River Gorge bridge in Virginia, where for one day every year jumping becomes legal, and jumpers literally queue for the chance to jump the several hundred feet to the valley floor, and on to a small clear area adjacent to the river. The event is quite tightly controlled. Pre-registration is essential, and a minimum experience level necessary before permission will be granted. Professional and practical advice is on hand to prevent things getting out of hand, and although a high level of risk is obviously present, the safety record is such that the event has become as much a public spectacle as an experience for the jumpers themselves.

It is easy for some to condemn base jumping out of hand, and arguably it may not seem to have a place in a book that is devoted to the more mainstream aspects of the sport. It would serve us to remember, however, the exploits and ideas of the very earliest pioneers who, in the absence of aircraft, saw fixed objects as the only means to test and display their prototype parachutes.

HIGH-ALTITUDE JUMPING

Most routine skydiving happens from an altitude of 15,000ft (4,500m) or below. This is for several very good reasons.

- Above an altitude of around 12,000ft (3,500m) the amount of oxygen present in the atmosphere is greatly reduced. We all need a certain amount in order to function at peak level, and a deficit can impair our ability to think rationally and to co-ordinate our movements. A condition known as hypoxia arises from a prolonged exposure to the thin air of extreme altitude and can eventually lead to brain damage and death. The provision and regulation of on-board oxygen systems is an exacting and costly business, and outside the scope of most commercial drop zones.
- At these altitudes also, there is a sharp

temperature drop. Most skydivers in temperate climates are used to jumping 'sub-zero' throughout the winter time, but the clothing required to protect one-self at extreme altitude is not readily available to most jumpers.

- Piston-engined aircraft are approaching their operational ceiling at these altitude, and for even a turbine to fly consistent lifts to high altitude would extend the 'turnaround' time to an unacceptable length for a commercial centre.

Usually when recreational skydivers venture above their normal jump altitude it is to pursue a formation record: the extra time in free fall is necessary simply to get all participants in the same piece of sky at the same time. But even in these instances, the altitude is limited because the oxygen supply is only available on board the aircraft, and not as a personal unit for each parachutist in free fall.

Only the military venture to high altitude on a routine basis. Special forces parachutists are trained in HALO ('High Altitude Low Opening') techniques. This specialized form of skydiving is used to insert small units of troops behind enemy lines undetected by hostile ground forces. Usually this will be for intelligence-gathering purposes, or sometimes to establish a safe drop zone for large numbers of regular airborne troops to be deployed later by static-line descent.

Usually when a non-skydiver persuades a jumper to talk about the sport (not usually very difficult to do) not much time goes by before the invariable question of the highest-ever free fall. This honour goes to Colonel Joe Kittinger of the United States Air Force who, in 1960, jumped from a balloon gondola at an altitude of over 100,000ft (30,000m). The purpose of this incredible

achievement was not to break records; it was pursued as part of a programme to test escape and survival systems for pilots flying at high altitude. The problems associated with staying alive when you are above 98 per cent of the earth's atmosphere don't just relate to temperature and oxygen availability; there is also the need for a pressure suit to prevent the body's fluids boiling away as they are exposed to the hostile environment.

A pilot baling out at such altitudes would need to free fall down to an area of higher pressure and available air before opening a canopy. Bearing in mind that most parachutes are designed for an opening shock below 150mph (250km/h), and that Kittinger's terminal velocity would be in excess of 600mph (1,000km/h) due to the thin air, one can begin to appreciate the problems and the risks involved.

Another factor to consider was one of stability. We have seen how a skydiver uses the pressure of the relative air to shape their body and remain in control, but in extremely thin air, these principles simply don't apply. The Beaupre Multistage parachute system was developed to address this. Shortly after exiting the gondola, a timer would release a 6ft (1.8m)-diameter drogue chute that would inflate in the thin air and provide some stability. Eventually, a barometric device would sense the jumper's altitude and speed and fire the main canopy.

Kittinger made an initial high altitude attempt in 1959, from 76,000ft (23,000m). It almost cost him his life due to a premature initiation of the drogue timer sequence. The drogue, due to deploy sixteen seconds after exit in order to have the benefit of velocity for deployment, fired after only three seconds and wrapped around Kittinger's neck! The main canopy, attached to this, eventually fouled with him also, and he returned to earth under the reserve. He determined to repeat the attempt, and did so less than a month later. This time, all went according to plan and the main canopy opened at 18,000ft (5,500m), as planned.

Kittinger and his team decided to press ahead towards their final objective, a descent from in excess of 100,000ft. This altitude was regarded as a benchmark for the test programme. Kittinger stated:

> We thought that from 76,000ft, if any part of the pressure suit malfunctioned, the pilot *might* have a chance to survive. That he could fall to a safe environment before a malfunction produced a fatality. But from over 100,000ft, any error or malfunction would be critical. The height would preclude any chance of a safe return to a safe arena.

The final attempt was made on 16 August 1960, and from an altitude of 102,800ft (31,350m). It was entirely successful, if not without incident (a malfunction in his pressure suit caused damage and swelling to Kittinger's right hand). It is highly likely that this record will never be broken simply because the programme fulfilled all its objectives and the need is no longer there.

Countless pilots over the years have reason to be grateful to Joe Kittinger and what he himself describes as 'A brief visit to the shoreline of an alien world'.

STUNT PARACHUTING

All stuntmen and -women are required to have a parachuting qualification on their CV. However, few pursue the sport to the level needed to perform some of the stunts and exercises that we see in a lot of mainstream motion pictures today. Most of the James Bond films of recent years have included skydiving to some degree. It's all there up on the screen: fighting on top of aircraft, fighting in free fall, plummeting towards the earth without wearing a parachute of any sort! That particular illusion was achieved by wearing a harness and container system underneath a conventional set of clothing with a Velcro release on the back.

The men and women who perform these feats are experts in their field, for any stunt requires a meticulous degree of planning. Bear in mind that assumption of risk in these cases is far greater than for routine skydiving.

Afterword

Any skydiver who is questioned about their motivation, and the reason that they pursue the sport, will generally give a predictable answer. They will tell you that it is fun, or that it takes them away from the pressures and routine of their job. They will say that it gives them the opportunity to relax in the company of like-minded individuals.

It is improbable that they will talk to you in terms of spirituality, of making contact with a higher aspect of their consciousness. It would be pretentious to say that we skydive in order to achieve self advancement in this respect. However, there is something that we have in common with all others who invest their time in adventure sport. This something is an encounter with what I choose to call 'the now'.

For most of our lives, we carry out our daily tasks without total focus. That is to

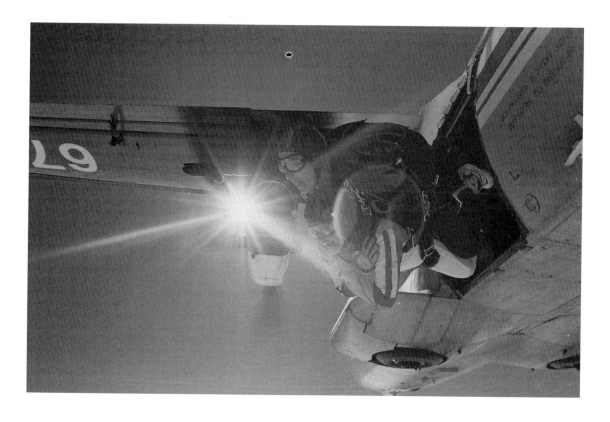

say that the worries and stresses that we all have, occupy a small part of our consciousness *all the time*. We might be lying on a beach or eating a nice meal, but still we find time to worry about our overdraft or our recent argument with the boss. The larger the worry, the more of our thinking time it demands.

It is only when our minds are so stimulated, so concentrated, either by exhilaration or danger, or a combination of the two, that we truly purge ourselves of unnecessary mental clutter. We live, for however brief a period, in 'the now', an 'out of time' state of mind that seals itself off from distraction. The bank manager will still be there when we land.

The concentration necessary to attack a rock face at the edge of your ability, the countless instantaneous decisions that you make during a fast downhill ski run, or the co-ordination of mind and body needed during a four-way skydive demand complete commitment from all the participants involved.

I believe that this 'purging ' is good for you, and is part of the reason for the exhilaration we feel after exposure to extreme environments. I think that skydiving, along with any true adventure sport, can reduce negative stress, by periodically imposing positive stress. As one realises this, the sport becomes addictive and we will want to repeat the experience as soon as possible.

Having said this, I do not think that anyone considering making a first jump, or an existing parachute student climbing the progression ladder, should look for any reasons beyond the fact that it is all just really good fun. Anyone able enough, looking for a little adventure in their lives, would be hard pushed to find a sport to match it.

Glossary

Anyone who chances to overhear a conversation between two or more skydivers may be forgiven for thinking they are hearing an alien language. The same is true of any complex, technical sport. Throughout this book, I have tried to explain terms and technical abbreviations as they have occurred. Here they are again in summary, along with a few that slipped through the net.

AAD Automatic Activation Device. A back-up system, historically mechanical, now more usually electronic, that compares ambient air pressure with descent rate and initiates reserve deployment at a pre-set height.

AFF Accelerated Free Fall. A method of teaching which aims to accelerate the learning process by prolonged exposure to free fall.

Altimeter A device used to read off altitude in free fall or under canopy.

Bag lock A malfunction of a free-fall system where the lines have deployed but the canopy is trapped in the deployment bag.

BASE Buildings, Antennae, Spans and Earth. Alternatives to aircraft!

BOC Bottom Of Container. Placement for a hand-deployed pilot chute.

Brakes Modes of flight for a ram-air canopy: half brakes, full brakes, and so on.

Bridle line/cord A line used to attach the pilot chute to the top skin of the canopy via the deployment bag.

Canopy Alternative term for parachute.

Container system A rig that contains main and reserve canopies.

Crabbing Facing a canopy across the line of wind direction.

CRW Canopy Relative Work. Flying parachutes in formation. Also called Canopy Formation (CF).

Cutaway The act of jettisoning a malfunctioning main canopy prior to opening the reserve.

CCI Centre Chief Instructor.

Debrief Post-skydive analysis. Sometimes apportionment of blame!

Delay The period of time spent in free fall.

Deployment The opening sequence of parachute.

Deployment bag A bag used to contain the canopy prior to deployment.

Disc The target in accuracy competition, 3cm in diameter.

Dive Swooping down to a free-fall formation prior to a final approach.

Docking Taking grips on a free-fall formation.

DP Dummy Pull. Learning to pull a dummy ripcord during a static-line descent as part of training for free fall.

Drop zone The area of ground on which parachutists will land. Also used to refer to the parachute centre itself.

Dump Slang term for initiating the opening of a parachute.

Exit The moment of release from the aircraft. Either for an individual or a formation.

Flare Technique used to land a ram-air canopy. Both steering toggles are pulled down together at the moment before landing, extra lift is created and the canopy slows to a desirable speed for touchdown.

Floater Position during a formation exit involving setting up outside the aircraft, hanging on a special rail.

Formation Group of two or more people linked in free fall.

Formation skydiving Two or more skydivers falling together in free fall. Also called relative work.

Free fall Portion of skydive prior to opening the canopy.

Funnel Slang term for the collapse of a free-fall formation, usually due to a poor docking. Results in individual skydivers falling through each other's wake turbulence. Chaos!

Glide ratio The ratio of forward movement to descent rate under canopy.

GPS Global Positioning System. Computer system that cross-references satellites in space to confirm a ground position. Used to position aircraft over the opening point at high altitudes.

Grip Handle on a jumpsuit arm or leg. Used to hold during formation skydiving.

Groundrush Apparent acceleration of the ground below during free fall. Speed seems to increase with proximity, particularly when one is below a desirable safe opening altitude!

HALO High Altitude Low Opening. Type of jump used by special forces for covert troop insertion.

Hand signals Used during free-fall coaching by the instructor to communicate positional changes and other information to a student.

Hang-up An emergency situation resulting in a parachutist hanging underneath the aircraft after exit. In a student context, usually the result of a fouled static line. The student is cut free and then deploys their reserve. Thankfully rare.

Harness Webbing assembly worn by a jumper as part of container system.

Holding Facing the canopy into wind. Has the effect of reducing ground speed.

Holding area An area of ground over which a student parachutist will stay under canopy to prevent them straying too far from the target.

Hook knife A small knife with a protected blade used by parachutists to deal with line entanglements and so on.

Hook turn A fast turn under canopy made at low altitude to generate extra speed and lift for landing.

Hop and pop Slang reference to a very short free-fall delay.

Inter A designated transition during a sequential formation skydive.

Jumpmaster A skydiver designated as being in charge of the organization and control of a lift of parachutists. In the case of students, the jumpmaster is always an instructor.

Kill line A concentric bridle cord assembly to collapse the pilot chute after full deployment of canopy. This reduces drag as the canopy flies.

Line over A canopy malfunction involving a line or lines that the canopy has attempted to invert through.

Malfunction Any situation after deployment where the canopy is not able to fly correctly, necessitating the use of the reserve canopy.

Night jump A skydive performed after dark. To be precise, more than thirty minutes after official darkness.

Opening point The point on the ground, upwind of the target, above which skydivers will open their canopies.

Opening shock The force felt by the jumper as the canopy opens. Can be affected by speed, body position or the way the canopy has been packed.

Oscillation Experienced under round canopies, less so under ram-airs. The jumper is swung from the vertical axis during a turn, increasing descent rate.

Packing The process of folding the canopy into its container prior to jumping.

Pilot chute A small drogue canopy, with or without an internal spring, used to create drag and deploy the main canopy.

PLF Parachute Landing Fall. A method of bracing the body prior to landing and rolling across the back. Used routinely under round canopies, or as a contingency under ram-airs when a hard landing is inevitable.

Poised exit Any release from the aircraft that involves a jumper facing the direction of flight, such as sitting in the door or standing on a step above the wheel.

Porosity The amount of air that will pass through a given area of canopy material. Expressed as a percentage.

Premature opening A deployment that occurs accidentally before the jumper has intentionally initiated it.

Pull-up cord A short length of line used to close a parachute container.

Rating A qualification in parachuting. Advanced instructor rating etc.

Relative work *see* Formation skydiving.

Reserve Auxiliary parachute for use in the event of a malfunction of the main.

Riser Webbing straps rising from the canopy attachment point to the suspension lines.

RSL Reserve Static Line. A back-up device attached to the riser of the main canopy which pulls the reserve ripcord pin after a cutaway.

Running Facing the canopy downwind. Has the effect of increasing ground speed.

Slot A skydiver's designated place in a formation.

Spot The opening point.

Spotting Directing the aircraft towards the opening point prior to exit.

Stable position The spread, arched position adopted by skydivers to achieve control in free fall. Usually this is a face-to-earth position, but can refer to any body position that can be maintained under control.

Static line On student parachute assemblies, this is used to deploy the main canopy. It remains attached to the aircraft as the student falls away and pulls the deployment bag from their container.

Swooper One of the last skydivers to dock on a free-fall formation. So called because of their late exit position and the necessity of a prolonged dive down to their slot.

Target The intended landing area.

Terminal velocity The maximum speed that a body can achieve in free fall. Terminal velocity varies with body position and weight. It is reached after approximately twelve seconds in free fall.

Tracking A free-fall body position that maximizes horizontal movement. Used to gain separation after formation skydiving.

Water jump An intentional descent into water. Usually seen in a display, or performed to gain ratings of some sort. Always organized with adequate rescue infrastructure.

WDI Wind Drift Indicator. A roll of brightly coloured paper with a weight at one end that is thrown from the aircraft by the jumpmaster. The subsequent drift is used to determine the opening point.

Whuffo Slang for a non-jumping spectator. 'Whuffo they jump out of aeroplanes?' This expression has always seemed rather daft to me.

Windsock Large tubular flag used to indicate wind direction.

Zoo Slany expression used by skydivers to refer to any skydive that has gone spectacularly wrong. As in 'That was a complete zoo, don't ever jump with me again!'

Further Information

FURTHER READING

Hearn, Peter, *The Sky People* (Airlife, 1990)

Frensch, Thomas, *Skydiving Book* (Anderson World Inc., 1980)

Poynter, Dan, *Parachuting – The Skydiver's Handbook* (Parachuting Publications, 1978)

USEFUL ADDRESSES

UK
British Parachute Association
Wharf Way
Glen Parva
Leicester
LE2 9TF

Tel: (0) 116 278 5271
Fax: (0) 116 247 7662
www.bpa.org.uk
skydive@bpa.org.uk

Skydive magazine
3 Burton Street
Peterborough
PE1 5HA

Tel: (0) 1733 755 860
Fax: (0) 1733 755 860
www.skydivemag.com
editor@skydivemag.com

USA
United States Parachute Association
1440 Duke Street
Alexandria
VA 22314

Tel: 703 836 3495
Fax: 703 836 2843
www.uspa.org
uspa@uspa.org

OTHER SKYDIVING WEBSITES

Federation Aeronuatique International
www.fai.org/~fai/parachuting

Australian Parachute Federation
www.apf.asn.au/~apf

Paramag (France)
www.home.nordnet.fr/~paramag

Skydive Net   www.skydive.net

Skydiving Images – Norman Kent
www.normankent.com

Skydiving Images – Keith Larrett
www.visexp.com

Yahoo Skydiving links
www.yahoo.com/Recreation/Aviation/Skydiving

Appendix: The BPA and USPA Licensing Systems

All sport parachute centres in the United Kingdom and the majority of those in the United States are affiliated to, and operate in accordance with the operations manuals of, the British Parachute Association and United States Parachute Association, respectively. What follows are simplified introductions to the rating and licensing systems used by the two associations.

THE BRITISH PARACHUTE ASSOCIATION

Student parachutists progressing through the BPA training system are classified in eight categories, Category 1 being awarded when the student is trained and ready for his/her first static-line descent and Category 8 on completion of the training syllabus, when the student has demonstrated the ability to make safe solo freefall descents, including manoeuvres such as turns, backloops and tracks. Students training under the AFF system are awarded Category 8 on completing the AFF syllabus and doing at least ten solo 'consolidation' jumps.

There are then a number of further qualifications to be achieved in the various disciplines of the sport: Individual Canopy Grade 1 (IC1) is a basic qualification following on from Category 8, including basic accuracy and spotting; Formation Skydiving Grade 1 (FS1) is the basic FS qualification; Individual Style Grade 1 (IS1) the

basic Style qualification; and so on.

These BPA-specific qualifications entitle the parachutist to the internationally-recognized parachutist's certificates awarded by the Fédération Aéronautique International (FAI), which are now needed for a parachutist to be recognised by the BPA as an intermediate or experienced parachutist, rather than as just a student. The requirements are as follows:

FAI 'A' certificate: Category 8;

FAI 'B' certificate: 'A' certificate, at least 50 jumps and IC1;

FAI 'C' certificate: 'B' certificate, 200 jumps and at least one additional Grade 1;

FAI 'D' certificate: 'C' certificate and 1,000 jumps.

All parachutists below 'A' certificate level are classed as student parachutists; all 'A' certificate holders are classed as 'intermediate' parachutists; and all parachutists with a 'B' certificate or above are classed as 'experienced' parachutists. The certificate held by a parachutist has some bearing on what he or she may do in the sport. For example, an 'A' certificate holder may not act as the Jumpmaster in charge of a lift; and a 'C' certificate is the minimum requirement for a parachutist to commence training as an instructor.

It should be borne in mind that the current rating system was introduced as recently as 1998, prior to which the requirements for each FAI certificate were less stringent – for example, the requirement for a 'D' certificate was roughly the same as the current one for a 'C' certificate. To avoid confusion, FAI certificates issued under the new system are red and have six-digit numbers, whilst the certificates issued previously are blue and have numbers of up to five digits.

UNITED STATES PARACHUTE ASSOCIATION

The USPA issues 'A', 'B', 'C' and 'D' licences, recognized by the FAI, for which the requirements may be summarized as follows:

'**A' Licence**: twenty freefall jumps and at least five minutes' accumulated freefall time

'**B' Licence**: fifty freefall jumps and at least ten minutes' accumulated freefall time

'**C' Licence**: 100 freefall jumps and at least twenty minutes' accumulated freefall time

'**D' Licence**: 200 freefall jumps and at least one hour of accumulated freefall time.

In addition, for each licence an increasing proficiency in formation skydiving, style and accuracy must be demonstrated; at each stage a written text must also be undertaken. Qualification for the 'A' and 'B' licences each require training to be undertaken for landing in water, and for the 'D' licence at least two night jumps must have been made.

Index